Yet Another Existential Crisis

Jacob A.L. Martinez

ISBN: 1975931653
ISBN-13: 978-1975931650

To The All-Stars

This book is dedicated to Ms. Beltran and her second period class (from 2016-2017) whose names are listed below:

Jasmine Anderson
Mason Brown
Matthew Brandsen
Thomas Corvi
Andrew Fisak
Amelia McBride
Martin Casas
Conner McCully
Matthew Dorgan
Jordan Flores
David Folsom
Lucas Fowler
Sally Gietzen
Val Gillcrist
Kyle Grady
Fiona Harris
Josephine Hart
Clifford Haywood
Amanda Johnson
Anthony Karty
Grayson Kelle
Miles Koupal
Rio McLellan
Maya Nielsen
Rosa Perez-Granados
Brayden Quesada
Brendon Reperttang
Augustus Schrader
Samantha Smith
Ava Stevenson
Trevor Sykes
Bailey Turner
Thania Amador
Colette Huber

And, of course, Yolanda Beltran.

Every word that I think, speak, and write is because of you.

Table of Contents

FOREWORD

Jacob Martinez - simply a name on a class roster of 36 new students. Another list of names, another year of teaching, another opportunity to make an impact on young people…or so I thought. As it turns out, this one name - attached to this one soul - became an opportunity to make an impact on me and countless others.

Jacob is a different sort of soul – the kind of free spirit that misses the second day of school but not the first. He is the type of kid who wears salmon colored pants with a button up covered in hot dogs. He is the type of kid I wanted to be in high school – effortlessly cool without even trying.

High school has a way of "normalizing" the average – making the "normal" so very, very typical. The outliers are the "weirdos" – the teenagers who don't wear messy buns and yoga pants or skinny jeans and sip lattes. So I guess Jacob is a "weirdo", but it's not due to his clothing of choice or the physical meatsuit he inhabits. (Though it should be noted that his sense of style is, in fact, extremely enviable.) Jacob stands out because he can put into words the commonality of our human experience. His words paint a vivid picture of loss, of hurt, of happiness found in the most unexpected of places. He makes his readers – young, old, and everywhere in between - feel seen, heard, recognized. And he's barely just begun his own journey of life.

Decades younger than many accomplished writers, Jacob has a voice that reverberates. He has a voice that speaks to the thoughts many of us carry around bottled up inside. The thoughts that percolate and make us each wonder if we're the only ones thinking such things. He does with his words what most of wish we could do – he speaks them, he writes them, he gives them life.

Whether a fictional piece or a witty recounting of an actual life event, every word Jacob pens pulls us closer to one another in this experience of life. And what this fractured world needs is more people like Jacob who are willing to be brave enough to tell the kind of truth that brings us together.

If all you get the chance to read is "The Black Magic Breakup", a genius missive about a traumatic breakup, you will garner great insight into the luminosity of this writer's mind. He spreads the light of a thousand splendid suns with each consciously chosen word.

And what a gift that is.

Love and Light,

Beltran

KLEPTOMANIA

Like most people, whether they admit it or not, I have stolen something. Upon reading this, some people's eyes will grow wide in shock, and their mind will fill with the worst situations imaginable. Try not to think less of me, because I was young and stupid. Or at least, that's the excuse I use.

My criminal career began in preschool, just a few days after I had gotten my one and only Barbie. She was blonde, beautiful, and already missing a shoe due to my constant removal and addition to her outfit. The lack of clothing options I had available was the worst thing a 4 year old could imagine, so after my constant begging proved futile, I resorted to something far more drastic.

The preschool I went to was small, with only 30 kids split into two classes. Our play area consisted of swings, tires, a concrete track for tricycles, and way too much sand. In the far back corner, next to all the shovels and bikes, stood a small shack that one special child got to visit each week. That sounds like the premise of a horror film involving child sacrifices or manipulative psychopaths, but in reality, being chosen to go in was the highlight of every kid's very short life.

The reason we went in was to get a free new toy from the very small box in the center of the room, which was slowly overflowing due to the amount of items being forced into it. I took notice of this overabundance of rewards, and took it upon myself to fix the problem. Trust me, it was a noble cause.

I slowly began to steal toys from the box every day, usually hiding them in my shirt so no one would notice. I probably stole around 50 things total before I went to kindergarten, and I probably would have stolen more if my greed hadn't caught up to me.

Just like any other day, I entered the shack alone, and began to dig through the box. I already had plenty of accessories by this point, so I decided to try and steal some furniture instead. This was a horrible mistake, because the clear purple chest I wanted looked like a very dangerous square tumor when hidden under my shirt.

Obviously, I was spotted immediately, and after crying for a few minutes while my teacher scolded me, I was asked, *Have you taken anything else?* I was always told lying was bad unless it was for a good cause, and luckily for me, I believe accessorizing is a great cause, so I shook my head no.

After that, my teacher smiled, told me to never do it again, and took the box from me as I hid a stolen piece of toy food behind my back.

My stealing spree began once again during the summer, while my family and I were on vacation in Paris for what was probably the 100th time. It was hot, and we were probably extremely tired due to the minimum amount of exercise we had forced ourselves to take part in.

Naturally, the only solution to such a problem is ice cream, so we all quickly walked into the nearest ice cream parlor that had working air conditioning and sat down. My brother ordered pear, yes *pear*, ice cream, my parents got plain vanilla, and I decided to experiment by getting a strange Spongebob popsicle, which sadly, did not taste very good.

As we were leaving, I noticed a very large poster lying on the floor, right next to a hook that had been clearly holding it up before we had arrived. On it, was the same Spongebob popsicle I had gotten, right next to the man himself smiling as the words "Bob L'éponge" hung over his head.

Since I am a mastermind criminal, I quickly formed a plan in order to steal this poster that was almost a head taller than me. The plan consisted of the following three steps:

1. Pick the poster up off the floor.
2. Take it with you.
3. Keep it.

Just as I had expected, my plan worked, and I managed to bring the poster all the way back to the apartment we were staying in. My parents, finally noticing I had taken a very large wall decoration, took the poster from me, looked at it for awhile, and then put it in my suitcase.

To this day, it is still hanging up in my room.

My final heist took place a few years later, in a small house somewhere in San Francisco. By that point, I had assumed I moved past my criminal ways. But old habits die hard, and before we left, I took something.

The house itself was bland, with most of the walls being a plain white and there being a strange lack of light despite all the numerous windows. Despite this, there was one large redeeming factor. The toys. Specifically, legos.

There must have been at least 15 drawers completely filled up with various lego pieces, sets, and characters. Like most kids that age, I believed that legos were the best things in the world, and even today, when surrounded by thousands of pieces, it's hard not to. I never wanted to leave, and if no one else lived there, I probably wouldn't have.

But alas, I did, and the day before we hopped in our car and drove home, I took one last look in each drawer. Inside one of them, was a lego shuriken, small enough to perfectly fit in my hand. I'm not sure why, but I desperately needed to keep it, so while no one was looking, I snuck in into my coat pocket.

I ran my fingers over the dull points over and over again during the car ride home, feeling worse and worse every time. My guilt had caught up to me, and I felt horrible for taking something that I could have simply asked for from my parents. The minute I got home, I ran to the backyard with tears running down my face, and buried it.

If I claimed my days of stealing were over, I'd be lying. I do still steal, though it's more of as a joke now than anything else.

Whenever a friend or even just a somewhat close acquaintance puts their phone down on the table and turns away, I reach over and grab it. I always just hide it somewhere dumb until they notice, and if they don't, my conscience makes me give it back to them anyway. The thrill of taking something you're not supposed to is strangely controlling, but weak enough where I'm able to make the right decision and always give back what I take.

So if you see me around, just remember to stay alert. Because who knows what could go missing next.

THOUGHTS

1/17/16

I'm going to start writing in this occasionally, I think.

[Roughly 20 smiley faces]

I hope this works.

THE WALL BALL COURT

I didn't have very many long-term friends growing up. There were a few exceptions, but for the most part, everyone who I would call a "friend" would only stay around for a couple of weeks before we both moved on to other people. This was fine with me, because I knew everyone in my class already, so we could all just talk whenever we got lonely or just didn't have anyone else to play with.

This completely changed in 4th grade, when I became long-term friends with 6 other kids, who we'll give different names for the sake of preserving their identities. They were:

1. ZZ: A black-haired Jewish boy who cared a lot about the environment.
2. Olive: A tall girl with short reddish hair.
3. Daisy: A shorter girl with blonde hair who also happened to be the youngest girl in our class.
4. Fire: The tallest kid in our class, with dark brown hair, an intellectual's

mind, and the beginning of a gut.

5. Rob #1: A kid almost as tall as Fire, who liked to play games and told enough jokes to keep everyone entertained for hours.
6. Rob #2: An Asian boy with glasses, strict parents, and a very bad temper.
7. Me: The oldest kid in the class who never did his math homework.

We all first talked to each other for more the five minutes at ZZ's new club, which was all about protecting the environment. During that first meeting, we all got acquainted, discussed out waste of water, and watched Rob #1 play Minecraft on the computer, which would later re-ignite my passion for video games and creating.

For the first few weeks, that was all we did, until one day, when roaming around the playground, Fire waved me over to where everyone else was playing. He invited me to join in on their wall ball game, which I had never played before, and I accepted. I didn't realize it then, but this court was where I would spend the rest of elementary school.

The wall ball court served less as a game area and more as a unifying force for the 7 of us. It's where we all became friends and maintained our friendship, so to better summarize those connections I made, I'll split up those stories in terms of both grade and person.

4th Grade:

ZZ was the closest friend I had in the group, at least at the time, and we showed that friendship through an equal amount of insults and friendliness. He was the head of our club, and was so passionate that it was able to rub off on everyone else and started our own personal environmental movement that didn't get very far.

For his birthday we all went to the beach with bags and sticks, and for the next 3 to 4 hours all we did was pick up trash and talk. It was honestly a lot of fun, and once we had all returned to his house, which happened to be only a couple blocks away from mine, we retreated into the alley behind it and began playing wall ball once again.

Out of everyone, Olive is the person who I remember the least about. Not because she was boring or anything like that, but because she was what you expected of her. She was smart, kind, had pale skin, and ultimately served as the anchor of our group. She kept us from drifting, but in a way, also stopped us from moving forward.

Still, the group wouldn't have been the same way without her, and I'll never forget how much she cared about every one of us.

Daisy, despite looking like an innocent and kind school girl, had the fury of a thousand suns. She was the shortest and youngest of all of us, with practically white hair and piercing blue eyes that were usually used to glare. We didn't know each other very well in 4th grade, for no other reason than that we didn't need to at the time, but there are a few interesting stories that I remember from back then.

For example, after our teacher was finished reading to us one day, we all got up from the rug in the front of the room and went back to our seats. Everything was quiet for a good 30 seconds, but then one kid yelled out: "What *is* that!?" and we all quickly turned our heads to where they were pointing. There, right in the center of the rug, was a gigantic white bra bigger than all of our heads. No one knew where it came from, and to this day, I still don't know the truth, but plenty of people claimed it was Daisy's, so for the past 7 years, I've just assumed it was hers.

Another time, I made the horrible mistake of doing one of the most rude acts one can do to anyone towards Daisy. I pointed at her. Not behind her back, but two feet away from her for a reason I can't remember. She told me pointing was rude, and after I didn't stop, she stepped forward and bit my finger. It hurt, and she tried to defend herself by saying her teeth were not meant to actually connect with my finger, but I think it's funnier to think of that as a lie.

Fire, unlike Daisy, tended to be very calm despite his larger size. He used his brain first and foremost, then his arms to hit a wall ball, and lastly his mouth to occasionally eat paper. Besides that though, there isn't much to say about Fire except that he was great friends with Rob #1, and played Minecraft with him on occasion.

Rob #1 was the funniest person in our group, often telling everyone else jokes while we waited in line for our turn to play. I became friends with him quickly as well, but at that point knew very little about him besides him having a younger brother who is one of the most adorable people you can ever have the pleasure of meeting.

He was more into sports than the rest of us as well, which tended to give him an unfair advantage while playing.

Rob #2, however, was completely different from Rob #1.

They had the same first name, yes, but Rob #2 was much shorter, had worse eyesight, and didn't tell nearly as many jokes as Rob #1 did. He was the most enthusiastic about wall ball though, often being the first one to grab the ball before the rest of us had even made it out onto the blacktop. I also distinctly remember him eating an unhealthy amount of snot in 2nd grade, but since I used to eat playdough, I'm not going to judge.

Finally, me. Despite being the newest member of the group, and now the oldest, I was quickly accepted as one of them and began playing with them every single day. I was horrible at wall ball at the beginning, but as time went on I was able to pick up a few tricks from everyone else which helped me catch up in a decently short amount of time.

I spent time with them at recess, lunch, and after school so much that they became the only people I talked to for the rest of 4th grade. Together, we all made a great team, and even better competitors.

5th Grade:

5th grade was mostly the same as 4th. Sure we had a new teacher, but she was right next door to our last one, and the only new things she did was dissect a lizard and show us pictures of her colonoscopy. The wall ball wall didn't move though, and neither did the ball rack, so when it came to entertaining ourselves, nothing changed.

Despite ZZ being my closest friend in the group still, I bullied him constantly. I'm not sure what twisted part of our minds made everyone just accept it, but I was full on vicious to him. There would be the normal joke insults I would say to him and we'd all smile, but then I would also push him over onto the hard ground multiple times a day.

Everyone thought this was hilarious, including ZZ, so I just kept doing it over and over again. I have actual video evidence on my computer of me pushing him over in my house so quickly that he disappears from sight in a second and makes a huge crash that is quickly cut off by the sound of the two of us laughing.

It's either horrifying or spectacular, and I'm not sure which.

Olive, once again, remained how you would expect, with one simple twist. We discovered she was terrified of Elmo. We used to invite her over and set up ZZ's Elmo doll he would borrow from his sister in the most random places just to see how much we could scare her. There's even an old video of me and ZZ destroying the same doll on Olive's birthday, along with Frank's help. Frank being Olive's clear, glitter filled ball that we always had around.

Daisy and I were placed into the highest reading group in our class together that year, along with Fire, where we read amazing books that I still consider some of my favorites to this day. I'll never forget us sharing tears at the end of "Where the Red Fern Grows," or being shocked at all the clues in "The Westing Game."

In fact, "The Westing Game" became an inspiration to our whole group. We each decided which character we wanted to be, and then pretended to be them for hours on end. I wanted to be Christos Theodorakis, the 15 year old in a wheelchair, while Daisy wanted to be Turtle Wexler, who was pretty much the main character and always kicked people in the shin. It was a very fitting role for her.

I became much better friends with Fire this year than I did the year before, mostly due to me finally getting my own copy of Minecraft. Talking to him became genuinely entertaining and I felt smarter, for the most part, after each conversation. There was one moment, however, where during a high-five he missed my hand and hit me right in the face. Later that night when looking in the mirror, I noticed that his finger nail had left a dent that didn't go away for a week.

We never lived that down.

Rob #1 stayed the same. There's not much more I can say than that.

Rob #2 though, did go through a few changes.

He started getting more angry in 5th grade probably due to parental pressure, and often lashed out at the most random of times, like when at my house, he threw a giant rock so hard that it split in half. We still have it in our front yard.

His obsession with wall ball grew as well, leading him to, at one point, skip class so he could get to the wall ball court before everyone else. Naturally, our teacher was furious, and we were all confused as to why he would do something so stupid when he usually handled everything involving school so perfectly.

Together, we entered into Science Olympiad alongside everyone else in our group, me and him specifically going into a competition where we had to recreate something using only vague hints. It was during this event when I met his dad, who yelled at us for having fun instead of focusing, which ruined both of our moods. We ended up coming in 22nd place, and I blame Rob #2's father for that.

Wall ball still remained a vital part of my life till the end of that year, when we all had to move forward into middle school. While Fire, Rob #1, and I were staying at the same school, everyone else went somewhere else, and despite me hanging out with ZZ once or twice after that, it effectively ruined all of our friendships, as well as the environmental club. I didn't even talk to Fire and Rob #1 much any more except when playing video games, and those moments were few and far between.

I wish I could do a where are they now section, but I'm honestly not sure what happened to everyone. I still see Fire and Rob #1, though we only share a few passing words and waves now. I know ZZ still cares about the environment and is now fighting for bees, and I remember seeing Daisy on the SDUSD website holding a violin once, but everything else remains a mystery as to what happened after 5th grade.

All I know is that when I entered middle school, I didn't have very many long-term friends.

THOUGHTS

10/20/16

I saw [ZZ] for the first time in a while today. It was weird.

He looks just like his dad which is such a strange thing to think about because he no longer looks like himself. My memories of him and him now are so drastically different that I just have no idea what to think.

11/13/16

What is everyone I was friends with in elementary school doing now? Are they better off than I am? Are they still friends? It's super selfish but I kinda hope that none of them talk to each other anymore because then it seems less sad that I don't.

DOUBLE BOUNCE

One of my neighbors, who we'll call Field, used to have a trampoline in his backyard. It was one of the expensive ones, with a giant net surrounding it and a small trampoline beneath it to make sure it would catch you if you managed to break through the first one. We spent hours on that trampoline, running around, pushing each other, and anything else we could think of. It was mindless, and I think that's why we liked it.

Field was younger than me, and also significantly smaller, so he would get my old clothes whenever I came over, and he would give me a share of his food that my family thought was 'too childish' for someone of my age to eat. It was mutually beneficial.

We followed a routine after our exchange, where we first went into the basement so I could watch him play Mario Kart, until eventually we raced each other to see who could get to his backyard first. I always won.

The only thing to actually *do* in his backyard was use the trampoline, so we used it for everything. The majority of the time I would watch him do flips, or he would let me kick an exercise ball at him until he eventually fell over. We called it 'kung fu kicking,' and while he fell over everyday, I never did.

Occasionally, we would waste gallons of water and shampoo by covering the trampoline with it and then sliding around until we were satisfied. It was incredibly fun, but like everything else we did, it was basically each of us doing something by ourselves while the other person was just there.

On the few days when the exercise ball was missing, or we didn't have any shampoo left, we just jumped. Over, and over, and over again in our own little sections of the trampoline. But sometimes when one of us made a misstep, and jumped a little too close to the other person, they would go flying in the air.

And it was something we knew we couldn't have done by ourselves.

THOUGHTS

Acronyms my friends and I made:

Highway: Hold it Gerald. Hi. Wow! A yo-yo!

Smiles: Sometimes Miley is loudly eating sandwiches.

Dark: Demons are rarely killed.

Bile: Boys I like exist.

Mystery: My young sister tries eating random youths.

Regular: Royal elites get unusually long animal robes.

Winner: Why is nobody negotiating every response?

Shark: Strange hamsters are ruining ketchup.

MS. SMOKE

When it comes to english teachers, you're never really sure what to expect. Every subject has good and bad teachers, but due to the very limited amount of required material to teach and the fact that english itself is a very broad subject, a good english teacher is usually amazing, and a bad english teacher is usually horrible.

And I have never met a teacher more horrible than Ms. Smoke.

And it has nothing to do with her teaching, I genuinely learnt a lot in that class, and every other kid I used to know in middle school has agreed that when it comes to what teachers taught us the most, Ms. Smoke is at the top of that list. But that doesn't make her a good teacher. *My* definition of a good teacher is someone who teaches and makes the class want to learn.

And I can say for a fact that no one wanted to learn in Ms. Smoke's class.

I entered Ms. Smoke's class on the first day of 6th grade already not expecting very much good to happen due to the few things my brother had told me. He described Ms. Smoke as:

- Old
- Mean
- Very anti-God
- Someone who has gotten liposuction

And, something that we all started to think a few minutes in:

- Someone who needs to retire.

We started the first day off by watching a very poorly put together video about boiling water that was meant to inspire us to be the best we can be and teach us that the small things make all the difference. No one cared, because we were all 12 or 13 years old and, like most middle schoolers, assumed that we knew better than everybody else.

Our attitudes and obvious lack of caring began a very fast downward spiral of Ms. Smoke's opinion of us, and in turn, our opinion of her.

I'll never forget the first time we all had to give a presentation in her class. We were required to provide a clear outline and I, as well as a few others, wrote it out on paper instead of typing it up. The respectful thing to do would be to ask for a typed version by tomorrow. The kind thing to do would be to accept it like it is and tell them to type it the next time they presented. Ms. Smoke did neither of those things.

Instead, she lectured us, took our papers, wouldn't let us present, and threatened to give us a 0. Me and 4 other kinds left crying, and by the end of the year, she had left everyone else in tears as well.

Ms. Smoke despised all of her classes, but she hated ours more than the others, as she commonly reminded us, because we were in seminar, and were supposed to be better than we were, and more mature than we'll ever be. The only place somewhat safe from her constant glares was the back row seats, so whenever I was lucky enough to be there, I glared at her.

And there is a surprising amount of things you can learn about someone by glaring at them.

For example, Ms. Smoke kept a medicine bottle on her desk at all times that she never opened, touched, or even acknowledged. I have no idea what it was for. She also liked to drink her "tea" a lot, though it was very obviously diet coke, since that was all she ever took out of her purse. And when I say drink, I don't mean through sips or a straw, but with a spoon, as if it was soup or cough syrup.

I also noticed that whenever she read something off the computer, she had to completely lean into it, which I'm assuming sped up her already declining eyesight. She'd smooth out her clothes when she thought no one was looking, keep her hair untouchable to anyone, even herself, at all times, and wore the same exact shade of bright red lipstick every single day. It complemented her pale, wrinkly skin.

When we entered 7th grade, we all hoped, and assumed, that we would have the other english teacher, Ms. Corder, as our teacher that year, but we didn't. I'll never forget the sad looks on all of our faces and the disgusted one on hers as she opened her door and told us to get inside. She'd later fall on her face outside our math class while we all watched, creating the only moment where Ms. Smoke was able to make any of us smile.

That year we watched the boiling water video again, did presentations again, though I didn't cry this time, and got yelled at again and again. Because of this endless cycle of pain, most of 7th grade was just like 6th, but there were a few moments that added some spice to Ms. Smoke's character.

Like the time the only african american person in my class, we'll call her Dare, broke one of her legs. She couldn't move without crutches, and it was a pretty hard time for her since not only did it restrict her mobility, but she was also a model, so she couldn't work. Ms. Smoke saw Dare sit down one day and lean her crutches against her desk, and like any good teacher would, she picked them up and *threw them across the room.* I'm not joking. We all had to watch, since we weren't allowed to get up, as Dare hopped to the other side of the class to pick them up. This happened twice.

Another great moment was when my very tall friend, who we'll call Oreo, was asked for his interpretation of the story we read. In the story a boy went fishing in a boat with his dog, but a storm happened, and the boy was in a coma while the dog passed away. Then the "ghost" of the dog showed up and woke him from his coma before leaving, so Ms. Smoke asked us if we thought it was the dead dog or just a random dog, before assuring us that there were no wrong answers.

Oreo said it was a random dog, and that, was the wrong answer. I'll never forget Ms. Smoke's eye rolls and wild head movements as she yelled at him while asking, *Oh so you just think it's a random dog? You think the kid wouldn't be able to tell it wasn't his dog? I cannot believe you think our creator would just send him a random dog!* And that was the weirdest thing I realized about Ms. Smoke that year, despite my brother describing her as anti-God, she sure did talk a lot about a creator.

Oh well, I guess she just changed her mind.

At the end of 7th grade we were all assured by the principal himself that we would have Ms. Corder next year, and we were all relieved, even after Ms. Smoke told us she wouldn't miss us and that she was glad we would be out of her life on the last day of school.

So imagine our horror when we came into school as 8th graders only to see that Ms. Smoke's name was on all of our schedules. She was surprised too, so surprised that when she said she didn't mean what she told us last year it didn't come off as even the least bit genuine.

I'm not lying when I say that 8th grade was the most eventful year of that class, and that was partially due to the two new troublemakers in our class and also the fact that things finally started changing up this year. We didn't even watch the boiling water video.

But still, things were already off to a bad start at the beginning of the september, when Ms. Smoke made two fashion disasters in a row. The first was when she wore her skirt with a zipper on it backwards, so the zipper was facing the front. I'll never forget the screams from everyone around me as the zipper pulled itself up so fast that Ms. Smoke only barely caught it. Twice. The second was when Ms. Smoke explained to us that she just can't go out without something on her lips, and so when she realized she had run out of lipstick that morning, she put mascara on her lips instead. She looked like a corpse, and it didn't help that my desk was right in front of hers.

The best part of the year was the entirety of december since, as her only 8th grade class, we got to design a christmas tree to be in a competition. The theme was holidays around the world, and we got chinese new year, even though we wanted easter at the vatican. Our design consisted of a dragon head and body, a snake body, rose petals, and probably something else. My team was in charge of the dragon body, which ended up being a terribly put together paper tube that was just as bad as everything else on the tree. Besides the dragon head of course, that was made by an actual artist, which by all accounts, was probably cheating.

This month was the most carefree time of our middle school lives, despite the tree deadline, and we enjoyed every minute of it. Well, most of us. One of the new troublemakers who transferred into our class wanted to go home so badly that instead of cutting rose petals, he took the scissors and slit his wrist. We didn't see him again for a few days.

After december had ended and we had unsurprisingly not won the competition, everything went back to normal, for the most part. We pretended to like learning, and Ms. Smoke continued to pretend that we enjoyed hearing about her personal life. We learned all about her dogs, and divorce, and her plane license in the weird gaps between our learning.

Then, near the end of the year, someone stole Ms. Smoke's mascara, broke it in half, and left it outside her classroom door. She was furious. For weeks, we had to listen to her complaints and accusations while she tried to convince us that she was going to get security cameras and a police officer in her class. Of course, she never did, but to be honest, I was kind of expecting her to.

When we reached the end of 8th grade, we knew that none of the teachers were going to be sad that we had to go, since we really were disruptive and out of control most of the time, but we still got the normal goodbyes. Ms. Smoke however, didn't give us a normal goodbye. Ms. Smoke cried. And through her sobs she told us that somehow she had come to like us and that she was going to miss us next year. She even made every single one of us a personalized bookmark that was just a bit too big. I still have it with me, and sometimes when I'm alone, I'll look at it and think about how I might not have really known Ms. Smoke at all.

And I'll never forget that.

THOUGHTS

Notes I wrote in my phone after 1 am:

  Large French Fry

+ Medium French Fry

+ Medium Coffee

= $6.66 at McDonalds

———

Some boys be like "catch these hands" but I'm like "catch these lips."

———

Are you poopy get some soupy

———

You need clothes, but maybe not.

———

These aren't your onions

———

If you split up Yosemite, it sounds like someone who's bad at english telling someone named Sam to eat it.

Yo sem it e

MISS PALM TREE

In both 7th and 8th grade, I had the same science teacher, in fact, everyone at my school did. Her name was Miss Nye, she was short, had curly brown hair, and wore floral print dresses with dark leggings and tennis shoes, as if to show that she was only dressing nice because of obligation, but otherwise she had given up. This was backed up with her constant frown and quiet, bordering on whiny voice.

I'm not sure why, maybe because of how she looked and spoke, maybe because her classroom was the largest one, or maybe because everyone's horrible middle school mind connected when we sat on stools, but out of every other class, we all took Miss Nye's the least seriously. The majority of that class consisted of screaming, inappropriate jokes, bad grades, and Miss Nye getting angry. At the beginning, everyone was a terrible student, and I was not an exception.

On our first quiz, I got a 3 out of 16, and I went up to her after class to talk about it. Not because I wanted to do better, but because she forgot to give me half a point, so I should have gotten 3 ½ out of 16. My friends and I found this amusing, but Miss Nye just found it a little disappointing, and looked at the grade for a little bit before muttering, *Jake, you did so bad.* It sounded so painful, as if you just told a child their favorite toy was lost, and I felt so horrible that I made it my goal to do better from that point forward.

This was, surprisingly, very easy, and I quickly went from and F to and A. Along the way, my friends and I decided that Miss Nye was our favorite teacher, and we started annoying her like everyone else, but with kindness instead of screams. We looked forward to her class every day and even stayed in their after school, partially due to the craziness of it all but mostly due to her reactions.

And her reactions were great. Rather than using names, she usually referred to people as *Boy* or *Girly* in her high pitched voice which meant she was starting to get annoyed. Some other common responses to all the craziness was when she would tell kids they were *Outta their mind* or that they needed to *Stop flirting* with whatever person of the opposite gender they were talking to. All of her words were coated with a sense of built up hate that you would expect from a white, 30 to 40 year old middle school teacher.

But what did Miss Nye have to deal with? Well, besides the normal annoyance of a middle school class, she had the added bonus of our class's absolutely terrible hijinks. Some of it was what you would expect, like people throwing pens or moving around stuff, but other times it got a little bit weirder.

For example, one time, a troublemaker in our class, who we'll call French Fry, stood up on a table and screamed out his adoration for the Mormon God Mitt Romney, and then when told to get down, claimed that he was just expressing his religious beliefs. Another time he, very randomly while someone else was reading, screamed, *I HAVE A PENIS AND A VAGINA AND ONE TIME IT WENT INSIDE AND I SCREAMED "MOMMY!"* Which, as you can probably guess, did not go over very well with Miss Nye.

Funnily enough, lots of stuff happened while we were reading out loud, which was probably because that's what we would do for the majority of our time in class. Usually Miss Nye would pull a card with one of our names on it and they would be the next one to read, but one day we actually convinced her to let us choose. I'm not sure how we did it, but after each paragraph, with no pauses, someone else in the room would start reading without anyone trying to read at the same time. It was a practically impossible amount of flow, which is what made it so satisfying to be a part of. A few months later, while my friend Lane was reading, she got to a sentence that said, *All organisms need nutrients and living space*, to which we all, in perfect harmony, sang, *Living Spaces!*

I even did some stupid stuff in that class, like when I forgot to bring my scissors with me when I went across the room to return them. After that, I ran back to my table with my arms flailing as I shouted, *I'm an idiot!* over and over again. Then, two days in a row, I leaned back in my stool, which as you can probably guess, is a very stupid idea. The first time I fell and hit my head against a cabinet, but the second time, I pulled off something amazing. While the stool was falling, I put my legs in the middle hole of the stool and stood, letting the stool hit the ground while I was completely fine. Everyone stared at me for a few seconds before one of my friends asked me, *How the hell did you do that?*

Besides the occasional moment of acting out, which was usually very minor compared to what most of the other kids did, I was a good student, and so because of this, Miss Nye placed me next to bad kids in the hopes that I would rub off on them. It did not work. When she put me next to French Fry, I looked up dead baby jokes on my phone for him to read to the class. When I sat next to my first grade crush, we'll call her Judy, I covered her entire paper in smiley faces that I hand drew on with red marker while she was in the bathroom. She then got yelled at by Miss Nye after she threw my pen across the room.

I sat next to one specific boy, who we'll call Ham, for a surprisingly long amount of time since, I'm assuming, Miss Nye was hoping he would start actually doing work if I did it with him. However, all this did was create two backpack incidents, and one female one. The first backpack incident was when Ham wasn't working since he left his backpack on my side of the table, but when I tried to push it back to him Miss Nye yelled, *Jake! He needs to do it himself.* The second was when he would move my backpack everyday, which was getting annoying, so I hid in a cabinet and when my friend knocked, signaling he had arrived, I opened it and caught him red handed. The female incident was when one girl, who we'll call Jazz, got mad at Ham because he kept saying *Roasted!* Ham retaliated by saying it was how he felt when she did the cup song, and then she turned around to face him, with a completely red face, and screamed, *WE DON'T EVEN DO THE CUP SONG ANYMORE! LISTEN WITH YOUR EARS NOT WITH YOUR EYES!* before breaking into maniacal laughter.

The last bad kid I had to sit with, before Miss Nye figured out I wasn't making them any better, was one of the new troublemakers who joined our class in 8th grade. During one of the jeopardy games we would do in that class, he decided it would be funny to answer every question incorrectly. I did convince him to put down the right answer for the question on motion, but then he added *Push it down the cliff* as part of the answer, which made it so we didn't get any points. At least it wasn't as bad as the time my friend Poise saw the picture of a moth frozen in solid sap with the question, *What is this?* to which she screamed out, *A MOTH! IT'S A MOTH!* Everyone then turned to her and said, we know it's a moth Poise, we're asking what something preserved in sap is called.

She didn't speak for a week.

One day, my friend Lane drew a picture of a palm tree running away from a horde of random creatures and objects. We decided that the horde was our classes noise, and therefore, the palm tree must be Miss Nye. To us, she then became Miss Palm Tree. After becoming a palm tree, she became even more special in our lives, so we decided to honor her, and what better way to honor someone then write a musical about them?

The musical was called 'Miss Nye on Ice,' and it was about our class being trapped in her room and unable to leave until we learned about the 4 rules that were always on the board and responsibility, which she told us we needed practically every day. The "On Ice" part was because we were going to end the musical with Miss Nye being pushed onto the stage while sitting on a giant block of ice. As you can probably guess, the musical was never made, but we did come up with a great song list, it being:

- Outta Your Mind
- Mitt Romney
- First Period is Lonely (Sung by Mr. Q)
- Girly
- Stop Flirting (Love song)
- Detention!
- Our Dark Lord
- After School P.E.
- Shut up Thor!
- I Don't Feel Anymore (Sad song)
- Cancer Salad (Sung by Ms. Corder)
- I was Going to be a Chemist

- Curve
- I Hate the Science Fair
- Palm Tree
- The 4 Rules
- Responsibility

Some of the songs you may have questions about might be *I Don't Feel Anymore*, or *Cancer Salad*, or even *Detention!* and *Curve*, so I'll explain them quickly. When asking Miss Nye if she was sad about some random thing we heard on the news, she responded that she wasn't because she, *Doesn't feel anymore*. *Detention!* was because she was the only teacher in middle school who gave out detention. *Curve* was because she would grade her tests on a curve.

Cancer Salad is a little weirder to explain. Basically, another teacher who we would bother, Ms. Corder, would walk across the quad where we were sitting to eat her lunch in the teacher's lounge. Every single day she would have a salad, but during breast cancer awareness month, the box was pink. We all created a theory that she only bought the salads when it was that month, and then stockpiled them for the whole year. Thus the name, cancer salad.

Because Ms. Corder and Miss Nye were our favorite teachers, we desperately wanted them to sit with us at lunch. So, I pulled off the greatest thing I have ever done. I asked Miss Nye to sit with us at lunch after class had ended, but she said no, so I went over to Ms. Corder's room. There, I saw her throwing away a box, but I told her I would take it off her hands instead. It was zebra print and was painted gold on the inside, making it absolutely hideous.

I knew Miss Nye would love it.

So, I went back to her class gave her the box, which she thanked me for multiple times, and then I asked her if she was willing to sit with us now. She agreed, and then I went back to Ms. Corder's room. I asked Ms. Corder if she would sit with us, to which she said no because she hated our guts, so I then asked if she would if Miss Nye sat with us. She rolled her eyes and said okay, assuming it would never happen. One week later, while sitting with Miss Nye, I heard the door to Ms. Corder's room open, and I turned to her and smiled.

I have never seen someone look like they wanted to suddenly drop dead more than she did in that moment.

Near the end of 8th grade, we all decided that we needed to do *something* for Miss Nye, since she had been our favorite teacher for the two years since we met her. So after school one day, we all pitched in money and ran to the nursery near our school. Two of us carried it back as quickly as possible while the others got her out of the teachers conference she was in and brought her to the front of the school.

And there, in a little black bowl, sat her own personal palm tree.

THOUGHTS

12/13/16

In middle school, the history teacher I had in both 7th and 8th grade was considered the best teacher in terms of people *actually liking him.* [We'll refer to him as Mr. Q]

During 6th grade, our history teacher was an incredibly smart woman who made learning enjoyable if you paid attention, all while being lenient when necessary and still managing to make everyone do well. She was a perfect teacher, at least, for her subject. And so at the end of the year when she announced that Mr. Q would be teaching us next year, we all let out a collective sigh in sadness, but quickly stopped when she told us he was an excellent teacher.

I think it would have been more accurate to describe him as a "great guy" but that's just me.

The main problem with Mr. Q was that he always wanted to be the "cool teacher" above all else, but that wasn't what he was supposed to be doing. Sure, technically he was just doing unconventional teaching, but sometimes things are done the way they are for a reason. Instead of having us read or telling us directly about knights and religion throughout Europe, he had us watch 'Monty Python and The Holy Grail,' which, in case you haven't seen it, isn't very historically accurate.

But I'm not lying when I say I enjoyed his class and him as a person, because how could I not? All he did was tell jokes and let us get 100% with minimal effort. It was a middle schooler's dream to be in that class, but now that I think back on it, I wish I was able to learn *something* during that time, rather that just write the word "death" over and over in my notebook to pass the time.

This is why I think the balance between teaching and having fun needs to be talked about more often. Some teachers make you *hate* learning, but others don't let you learn anything at all. Both are two sides of the same coin, and finding a middle ground is necessary if you want students to actually continue to learn after school ends.

But some teachers want all their students to like them, and as someone who has dealt with Mr. Q, who is possibly the most loved teacher at my old school, I can say with complete confidence that no matter how "cool" of a teacher you are, that is never going to happen.

THE BLACK MAGIC BREAKUP

If I could travel back in time and tell my 8th grade self one thing, it would be to stay far away from anyone who wanted to date me in middle school. Luckily, only one person had a crush on me back then, so avoiding them wouldn't be that hard. For the sake of preserving his identity, we'll call him Merlin. You'll see why.

I started 8th grade in early September of 2013. It was a simpler time, where all I had to worry about was how the other 58 kids in my grade felt about me, my rapidly growing depression, and the messed up schedules that took forever for them to fix. Like most people, I was ready to get middle school over with, so I could move onto better things like pursuing my interests, furthering my education, or finding a cute football player to date. I used to spend minutes upon minutes imagining the perfect guy for me to casually bump into. I'd drop my books, he'd help me pick them up, and after some really mediocre complaining he'd ask me for my number.

My friend Poise approached me while I was replaying one of these fantasies in my head, and with the charm of a sad Disney Channel star, she started to whine. *Jake, I have a secret I really want to tell you but I can't tell you!*

"Don't tell me then." I responded, trying to visualize the imaginary jock's smile as he handed me my last book.

Ugh! She groaned, *But I really want to tell you!*

"Okay then tell me."

But I can't!

"Alright then don't."

She stayed silent for a few seconds, probably trying to figure out what she should do. *Okay*, she smiled, *I'll tell you.* In her defense, she did keep the secret for 3 more sentences than I would have.

As it turned out, Merlin had a crush on me.

We had only talked a few times since we've known each other, each conversation consisting of a wide variety of boring topics no one cares about. He was a walking gay stereotype, with rectangular glasses, perfectly round black hair, and skin the color of a coffee bean after being left under a lamp for a few hours.

I wasn't attracted to him personally, or physically, but being your average closeted gay kid whose only sexual endeavors consisted of staring at Chris Redfield's biceps, I decided to ask him out. Around a week after deciding what to do, I told my friends I was gay, logged onto Facebook, and sent Merlin a message asking if he wanted to date.

He said yes, but I really wish he hadn't.

In order to offset the negative tone of this story, I'm going to take a short break, and make a quick list of everything *good* that happened due to me dating Merlin:

- It influenced me to come out to my friends.
- It influenced me to come out to my parents.
- He gave me some cool rocks one time.

That concludes my list of good things that happened because I dated Merlin. We will now return to your regularly scheduled program.

Things were already starting to go downhill right at the beginning. For starters, Merlin never wanted to go on any *real* dates. Instead, all we would do is message each other on Facebook as we comfortably sat miles away from each other. You'd think this would change at school, since hanging out with someone is completely normal, but it didn't. During our entire time "dating," we only spoke to each other in person twice.

The first time was in the boys bathroom after school, since he had told me a few days earlier to meet him there on friday. I, foolishly, assumed this would be where I would get my first kiss, so I furiously brushed my teeth and ate mints all week. This is when he gave me the rocks, and while I was disappointed then, I'm glad that he didn't actually try to kiss me.

The second time, however, was a bit different.

Instead of meeting in an empty bathroom that smelled like pee stained paper towels, we met on the blacktop during "The Halloween Carnival" that was always set up at our school. He had messaged me the night before, asking if I was going to be there, and when I said yes, he told me to meet him under the tree that they always set up the inflatable caterpillar next to.

Once again, I agreed to meet him, and after standing next to each other in complete silence for a few minutes, he handed me a piece of paper. It was a drawing of Eevee. The Pokemon. To be fair, it looked really good, but I was unable to say that to him in person, since he quickly ran away once the drawing was safely in my hands.

A few days later, I'm sitting outside during "The Halloween Dance" in what was definitely the most confusing costume there. I was minding my own business, wanting to be alone since no one understood what my costume represented except for my science teacher who I had explained it to. As luck would have it, my comfortable isolation was broken by Poise, who handed me a blue card while whispering, *It's from Merlin.*

Sadly, I no longer know where this card is, but I do remember that it was decorated with strings, beads, and had the entire inside completely filled in with text. If I had to guess, I would assume it said something like this:

Dear my lovely Facebook date Jacob,

I long for you. Everyday we are not together tears me apart inside. We do chat online, yes, but that is merely "dating," and does not reach the desired relationship I hope the two of us will share. As you know, I think you're rather smexy since you play tennis, so I, as well as many others, wish to be permanently with you. Forever.

Blah blah blah, I like your eyes, blah blah blah, I love you, blah blah blah, there are 3 more paragraphs full of everything I adore about you, my beloved Jacob.

Please be my boyfriend.

Please.

Love,

Merlin

Now how could I say no to such charming words?

My idea and Merlin's idea of what being boyfriends meant were drastically different. I assumed that the two of us would finally start seeing each other in public, hold hands, maybe share a milkshake, or even finally kiss. Merlin, however, thought that being boyfriends meant he could send me gifs on Facebook and occasionally give me his jacket, all while we were standing *at least* ten feet away from each other. If you're wondering how he gave me his jacket while standing so far away, it's simple.

He threw it at me.

As the months passed, I grew more and more annoyed with Merlin. Despite us talking every night, I still knew very little about him, and he knew even less about me. I desperately wanted to break up with him, but every time

I got close to doing it, I'd feel guilty. I kept putting it off day after day, up to the point where I worried that if nothing happened to break us up, I'd be with him for the rest of my life. Then one day, I got a message.

We need to break up.

"That's okay," I started to type, "I understa-" But before I could even finish typing, I got another message. 9 whole paragraphs that were clearly pre-written and then copied into the chat flooded my small phone screen. In order to save you from the pain I got, I'll summarize the story.

I'm very sorry Jacob, I know this must be hard for you to accept, but it must be done.

Over the summer something happened between me and my cousin. And no, it's not what you're thinking. It's just that both him and I have a strange similarity. We are both able to cast black magic, and after fighting for a very long time, he cursed me.

I'm no longer able to feel love, and I don't want you to be trapped with someone who is unable to return your feelings. I hope you can forgive me for leading you on like this.

I'm definitely not making this up.

Your ex,

Merlin

I did not respond.

Despite how much I despised it, for the next few months Merlin continued to message me on Facebook, and since I didn't want to be cursed myself, I responded. What follows are direct quotes from our conversations after we broke up. You have been warned.

JAKE

IF U HATE ME SO BAD

TELL ME IN THE FACE

U DUMB RETARD

"What?"

GET AWAY

I WILL STRANGLE YOU

"I don't understand why you want to strangle me."

hmph

u make it to obvious

"What obvious?"

if u hate me soooooo much

TELL ME IN THE FACE

Oh?!

YOU ARE A LIAR!!!!!!!!!

I ACTUALLY TOLD SOMEONE!

I DID EVERYTHING I COULD TO KEEP THE THING WE HAD

FROM FALLING

OH, BUT WHAT DID YOU DO?!

tell... me.....

what did you do........?

"You act as if I don't know I did nothing."

----

oh hey!!!!!

do you know katy perry!?!?!?!

"yes…"

oh, yeah?!!?

she's, like my celebrity crush!!!!!!

"Okay."

as stupid was your comment as mine that i just did now

"Cool. Anyways I have to go. Bye."

yeah yeah

shoo fly

don't think im happy with you right now, though

im still pissed off

REMEMBER THAT, RETARD!!!!!

"Can you stop?"

no shut up

"Stop please."

no

shut up

=.=

waaaahhh

"Are you okay?"

sniff sniff

no

Now after reading all those conversations you probably assume that I'm taking those out of context, but trust me, I'm not. In fact, there are way more weird things he's sent me on Facebook, but since writing out those conversations would be too long, I'll just summarize what happened.

Pretty soon after we had broken up, I got a text from my friend Rob #1, where he boldly asked *Are you gay?* To which I said yes and then proceeded to ask him how he had figured it out. Surprisingly, he hadn't. The reason he knew was because he got a text from an unknown number, which only said *Jake is gay.* I figured it was Merlin, but then after thinking for a while, I still couldn't figure out why he would even tell Rob #1 that in the first place.

But then Rob #1 gave me a hug in the park, and I got a furious message from Merlin.

y were u hugginh rob #1 after skool?!?!!

or y was he hugging u?!?!

I explained to him that it was just because we were friends, before asking him why he cared, instead of asking him the important question, which was *why were you watching me after school?* Merlin responded with these beautiful words:

uhuh

hes hawt.....

Wahhhh

And there we have it, Merlin's motive for texting Rob #1.

Another horrible thing that happened while messaging Merlin was that we did the worst middle school thing you could do, have a poetry competition. I'm going to spare you from reading my atrocious poems, since I don't want anyone to die from second hand embarrassment, but I also can't legally show you his.

Because he stole them.

The worst part about it was, that since they were so bad, I assumed he had written them himself, and I didn't bother searching for them online until I started writing this. The poems were properly named "Depressing Poem," and, "Angry Poem," among other horribly unoriginal names. But through my searching I did discover one poem that he had actually written himself. And yes, it is the worst one.

"Terrible Poem"

By Merlin,

hey hey hey

why duznt it rhyme rhyme rhyme

r u dumb dumb dumb?

repiti tion tion

You're a lie lie lie

You're gonna make me cry cry cry

Your insanity

Is distgusting me

But, hey, who am I to judge

Such a poor little bug

Who is struggling

To be in my glory

The final story, and arguably the weirdest, that I'll share with you, is one of the last conversations Merlin and I shared. I had known up to this point that he was depressed, not just because I was as well, but because he tended to mention it all the time. He even went as far as to bring it up every time he tried to get back together with me, and though I felt bad, I always said no. One day after receiving way too many depressing messages, he sent me this:

my masters body

he feels what i feel

i am merely a shadow

Naturally this confused me since it doesn't make any sense, but when I questioned him about it and his previous messages, he said:

i was feeling weak, so i slept for a while

i felt like...?

shadow... thing?

jake, wat u talking about?

those words....

i feel the same way

who was on my account?

I was furious after this. The fact that he not only destroyed the entire meaning of how he felt by turning it into a "real thing," but that the "real thing" was some stupid magic bullshit made me want to scream. I had continued to talk to him time and time again despite everything he said, but once he sent me:

I'm crazy

there's something wrong with me

I knew I couldn't take it anymore. I never responded to that last message, and I blocked him right after.

Merlin, if you are reading this, I want you to realize how horrible you were to me, and to yourself. You made elaborate stories instead of owning up to your own choices and feelings, to the point where it was hard to take anything you said seriously. I didn't have any romantic feelings for you, and it was wrong of me to ask you out simply because I didn't see another option, but it was terrible of you to criticize me when you had made just as many mistakes.

Going through our past conversations has hurt me more than I expected it to, and it's not just because of how cringy we were in middle school. I feel like I can't truly say how I feel without using your own words, and so, I will.

i was in a godd mood

ur stupidity has made me mad =.=*

THOUGHTS

[This is one of my old middle school poems. I'm sorry]

Forgotten Dreams:

In the field of forgotten dreams,

where no one ever sleeps,

In the field of forgotten dreams,

there grows a twisted tree.

The place where fairies grow,

and no one ever sleeps,

For the fairies evil glow,

that no one ever sees,

Forever holds a twisted smile,

so no one ever sleeps.

In the field of forgotten dreams,

there grows a twisted tree,

In the field of forgotten dreams,

no one ever leaves.

[Again, I'm sorry]

THE EAST COAST TRIP

At public schools on the west coast of the United States, there used to be a trip for 8th graders to allow them to travel to the east coast for a few weeks, that way they could learn more about the American Revolution and see the U.S. capital. However, due to America's fucked up economy and poor allocation of monetary resources, this program was cut before I entered 8th grade. However, I was lucky enough to have a school with teachers willing to spend their own, unpaid time to find a company that would be able to organize a trip for us, as well as join us on said trip as chaperones.

Since we could no longer get financial help from the school district to fund this trip, many students who were poor were unable to go, and those who could had to raise thousands of dollars to be able to. Me, as well as 10 to 15 other students, sold clothes and food in order to get minuscule amounts of money that went towards souvenirs, since our parents ended up paying for the entire trip instead.

Now, I'm not exactly sure *where* the trip started, since in all honesty, I only remember 6 different locations, and 3 of those are bus, plane, and hotel, so I'm going to assume we first landed in New York City.

New York was probably the most exciting part of the trip, mostly because of the hostile nature of those who live there, and so we started off everything in the most energetic way possible, by meeting up with another school since we couldn't afford to pay for a bus by ourselves. The other kids were nice, and we all talked with them as much as we could without it getting weird. I even met a girl named July, who became one of my best friends during the trip.

After we had all dropped off our bags in our rooms we began walking two by two throughout the city. There we saw great sights like, trash, smoke, and a billboard with a picture of a girl eating chips while wearing a shirt that looked *exactly* like the bag. I later emailed the company to see if I could buy the shirt, but, unfortunately, they don't sell them.

After eating what might possibly have been the worst veggie burger in existence, we split into two groups, those who wanted to go to times square, and those who wanted to go back to the hotel. I chose hotel, and I'm glad I did, because there were a few interesting events that took place that night. The first was when I found a Mormon Bible in our room, and I then put it in my backpack to read later, and the second was when my roommate Stalin and I cleaned Jim, a.k.a. the skunk skin Stalin had purchased earlier that still smelled like shit.

After we had finished, the kids in the room next to us asked us if we wanted to come over to their room to watch the soccer game. I don't like soccer, or any sports in general, but they were my friends and it was fun to sit in a small room with 5 screaming people. At one point they all got mad at Stalin and I because they discovered that we didn't have any other roommates. This was because, since Stalin had hearing aids, he and his roommate got to have their own beds since he has a disability. So while other kids slept on the floor or in the bathtub since they refused to share with each other, Stalin and I got to sleep comfortably without fear of physical contact. The only drawback was since our teacher's knocking in the morning wouldn't wake up Stalin, I had to violently shake him until he opened his eyes.

But back to the soccer game. While we were all watching TV, the two kids in the room next to ours started knocking on the wall, so we knocked back. Then they would run over to our door, knock on it, and then run back into their own room before we opened the door. This started a cycle of us knocking on their door, then them knocking on ours, until we eventually started leaving things like pieces of paper or pens outside each other's rooms.

Then after a knock and a nervous boy whispering, *Shit!* I opened the door and looked down, expecting to see some small object, but instead, saw that the hallway carpet was strangely wet. I smelled it and realized it was shampoo at the exact moment one of the chaperones exited her room just in time to see me on my knees with my face against the floor. The other kids in my room explained what happened, prompting her to bang loudly on our neighbors door to no reply.

She yelled at them the next morning.

On the very long bus ride to Pennsylvania, our two schools came together to perform a beautiful cover of 'Be a Man' from 'Mulan.' However, when we weren't singing, July would create scenarios for me and a few others to create stories off of. Every story was centered around Starthy and Nubbinson, who were characters created by my friend Field and I. They were lesbians, with Starthy being rich and a horrible person, and Nubbinson being an orphan who was sold to a drug company and tested on until she lost her arms leaving her with, you guessed it, nubs. Almost every story ended with Nubbinson dying, most of the time due to nub cancer, and in all honesty, I think that made them better.

When we finally arrived at Intercourse Pennsylvania, and yes, that is the real name, we quickly learned that we were there to learn about the amish lifestyle. After buying 'I Love Intercourse' socks and shirts from the gift store, we went to an amish family's shop. As it turns out, amish life is very different from how I was told. If you are amish and have a shop, you *are* allowed to have a phone and use cars for shipment, as well as have a working bathroom for visitors, which is very anti-amish in my opinion.

After having a decent meal of fried chicken and basically nothing else, I noticed that the amish children were riding scooters made from old bikes.

They were pretty cool, but it didn't make much sense to me to go through the trouble of turning an old bike into a scooter when you could just fix the bike. Since I didn't understand the reason behind it, I asked one of the amish women working nearby for clarification. She told me that it's because the children *can't leave us on a scooter*, which is probably one of the creepiest things someone has ever told me.

I was not sad when we had to leave.

Our last stop, that I can remember, was Washington D.C., where July and I decided to tell everyone we were cousins. Everyone, besides a few people, believed us, and my history teacher even gave us great advice that we *shouldn't have sex with each other*. Luckily, this was more funny than awkward, since July had already asked me if I was gay or not, and despite hardly anyone else in my grade knowing I was, I came out right away.

After taking a large group photo and dropping off the Mormon Bible at our next hotel, because I forgot to take it out of my backpack when we left New York, we all went on multiple tours of D.C., which to us, meant we were walking around for a few hours while talking. It was there where I told July that one of my favorite things to say as a joke was *Gag me with a spoon*, which caused her to then say it to the nearest boy in sight, prompting him to scream *NO!* and run away as quickly as possible.

While we all flew back to San Diego at the end of the trip, we made a stop in Texas to quickly drop off some people and pick up a few others. If you've ever flown on an airplane, you'll know this was not quick. We were stuck in that airport for hours, and I spent that time drinking four energy drinks, which was probably bad for my nervous system, and getting yelled at by one of the chaperones for drinking said drinks.

July, my friend Poise, and I all stayed up during the remainder of the flight, drawing out plans for our future weddings in our notebooks. When we did finally land, we went out to baggage claim to see our family's waiting for us. I followed July as she led me to her mom, where I was then given a hug and told I was the best nephew she's ever had.

To this day, there are still people who think we were really cousins.

THOUGHTS

(Sometime in late 2016)

I think it's sad to think about your old friends. I mean, I have great memories with them, and I want to see them again, but I kinda can't.

[Drawing of four sad faces]

At what point did me and my old friends just, stop speaking to each other? It wasn't a conscious choice, not on my part at least, so what happened?

The only thing that's worse than not seeing old friends is seeing them and realizing you have nothing to talk about. Like, I don't know this person any more. They're a complete stranger to me, even though I remember them laughing so hard their lungs hurt when I told a stupid pun on a bus one time, that's not them anymore. And I miss them, but they're gone.

THE GREAT BROWNIE HEIST

My friends Thor, Color, and I, spend the majority of our time together baking brownies in Thor's kitchen. By "our time," I actually mean Thor's time, since all Color and I do is stab the eggs and occasionally stir, although we do always help a lot with the taste testing, which is arguably the most important part.

Thor, however, decided that it was time for him to get his proper reward for doing all the hard work, so one day, while the brownies were baking, he waited for Color and I to go outside, and then he locked all the doors and windows so we couldn't get back in the house. He then proceeded to come out onto the balcony above us and announced that he was going to eat all the brownies by himself. Color and I laughed, until we realized he was serious and began to panic.

We must have checked every single door and window in that house at least 5 times before we gave up and decided to just sit on the bench under the balcony. But then I had an idea. It was stupid, and far too dangerous considering Thor's balcony was right next to a canyon, but I decided that the best course of action would be to climb up one of the balconies pillars since there was no reason for Thor to lock the doors upstairs.

I'm not sure what kind of fear consumed Thor when he saw my arms and face rise over the fence, but I can tell you that he did scream while Color and I both laughed.

Since Thor was impressed by our climbing abilities, we did get some brownies before he wrapped the rest of them up and put them in the fridge. We all watched a few movies together and talked, until eventually I noticed Color had gotten up at some point. I turned around just in time to lock eyes with her as she held a knife in one hand and the rest of the brownies in the other. I shook my head, told Thor I was going to use the bathroom, and got up.

She followed me into Thor's bedroom, where we then sat on Thor's bed, and proceeded to eat the rest of the brownies that we did not make. A few hours later, Thor's dad asked if he could have one of the brownies we had made earlier, and Thor agreed, until getting very confused as to where they could have gone.

Color and I could not stop ourselves from laughing.

THOUGHTS

1/4/17

My friend sent me a link to a live video of one of their friends who's going to fill a sock with ants and then put their foot in it.

Update:

He couldn't find any ants, BUT, he is going to eat a raw egg.

Update:

He is out of eggs.

Update:

He is going to put on a sock filled with thumbtacks.

Update:

We all voted for him to put it on his right foot, he did, and now he's in a lot of pain.

Update:

Another person in the live chat ate 54 thumbtacks and we all watched. [He actually only put them in his mouth and made it look like he ate them]

Update:

A random person came into the chat room, screamed "Why are you eating thumbtacks!?" and left.

Update:

Thor joined the chat and we all yelled at him for not seeing the one guy eat 54 thumbtacks.

Update:

Thor left.

Update:

The kid who ate the thumbtacks is now blowing up a whoopee cushion and talking about Bart Simpson.

Update:

The kid who ate the thumbtacks is now (literally) playing with fire, while the guy who filled a sock with thumbtacks is doing chemistry homework quietly.

Update:

I'm the only person left in the chat with the guy who ate the thumbtacks.

Update:

Guy who screamed and then left joined back in, asked when and how John Wayne died, and then left.

[He died in 1979 due to stomach cancer]

Update:

The guy who ate thumbtacks posted a picture of a girl completely covered in shaving cream.

Update:

I left the chat after about 2 hours. I'm very confused and extremely tired.

RUNNING MARATHONS

A marathon, by definition, is a running race with a distance of 42.195 kilometers. (26.219 miles) It's usually done on a road, however many are done on trails instead. It's extremely difficult, and if you know anything about me, then you'll know that any form of exercise that lasts more than 30 seconds is something I can't handle.

Sure, in the past I used to go hiking with my family for hours on end, but walking for 5 miles is a lot easier than running it. So then why do I run marathons? That's just it, I don't. I manage them.

Ever since I was 8 years old, my father has made me help him with his 3 main races, The PCT 50, Oriflamme, and The Peak, as well as others from time to time. All of these are controlled by Pinnacle Endurance, which my father runs and who I build websites for, so due to obligation, here's an ad: *At Pinnacle Endurance, we pride ourselves on hosting high quality runs that will stay with you for years to come. We currently offer 7 races. those being: Old West Trails 50K and 30K,*

Oriflamme 50K, PCT 50, The Peak Marathon and Half Marathon, and Stonewall Half Marathon.

As you can see, most of the races I help out with aren't marathons at all, they're 50 kilometer races, a.k.a., 31.0686 miles. Which, in case you can't tell, is *much harder* than a normal marathon. And, to add even more challenge, our races are on mountain and desert trails, meaning rocks, small paths, elevation, and heat. They are not for the faint of heart, even I'm tired after just working there, and I'm sitting most of the time.

When I was a little kid who had just first started helping my dad and didn't understand the terrors of reality, I assumed that one day I would run the marathons. But that assumption was almost immediately crushed after I saw how destroyed people were afterwards. People come in covered in dirt, sometimes bleeding, and desperately needing as much water as we can give them. Most are able to crash in a chair afterward and relax for 20 minutes until they leave, others have their legs give out and they have to sit with us for hours until they have enough energy to stand.

To this day people still gasp at me when I say I'm not and never will be a runner, and a few of them say that one day it will just come into my life like a revelation. I usually just nod, because it's better to not engage with crazy people.

That might seem offensive if you're a runner, but think about it from my perspective. We both wake up at 3 am so we can get to the race by 4 am, sometimes it's freezing cold and I'm wearing a jacket and am surrounded by 6 heaters, but you have on shorts and a tank top, the race starts at 5 or 6, and I wait at the start/finish for 8-14 hours for you to get back. The entire time you're running, or at least moving somewhat faster than normal, and you only get to refill your water and food supply at the 4 stops along the way. There isn't even a chance to sit down unless you want to drop out, and why would you do that when you could finish and get a pointless medal? Or, if you're fast enough, a small trophy.

Sure, I'm bored out of my mind and dying from the heat the whole time, but you're dealing with all of that while in constant fear that if you get off course at any point you could be lost forever because there is no cell reception out there. The only thing I have to deal with that you don't is you after the race, once you're all tired and hurt and complaining about how you'll never do it again. I know you'll come back next year, so I have to nod and nod until my neck hurts.

The rangers who have to monitor us are worse, but for different reasons. Since the trails are part of national parks, we have to pay for a permit to the race. So my dad sends in the check, the assistant fills in all the paperwork, and the director just has to stamp it. It usually takes 3 months for the director to do that, and by that point all of the money we gave them has already been spent.

The majority of the money goes towards the park ranger that has to watch over our races, which are so well organized that they usually sit in their cars and don't do anything the whole day, just to complain about having to work on a saturday. They get payed $79 an hour, and sometimes, they don't even show up.

My job at all the races is simple, in theory, since you can easily sum it up in a sentence. *When a runner comes in, write down their number and time, hand them a medal, and occasionally get them the shirt they forgot to grab in the morning.* However, you'd be surprised at how difficult and out of control this job can become. For starters, everyone's time needs to be written down to the second, which doesn't sound too bad, until more than one person starts coming in at a time and you have to quickly read all of their numbers, which they sometimes *hide* from you, and then remember who passed the finish line first and what second that was at.

This is also combined with giving out medals, which I guess everyone forgets exists, because you almost always need to chase down the runner with it after they cross the finish line. I'll never forget, or forgive my father, when I had to write down everyone's time, number, and give out their medals *by myself* when usually 6 people would show up at once. I was 10. After that, my dad realized that maybe there should be someone else who passes out the medals.

The only thing that's worse than that job, is something that happens consistently. The one, lone runner who refuses to listen to cut off times. It happens at every race, someone ignores the aid station's cutoff time and keep going instead of letting themselves be dropped out, for their own safety, and just keep going. They're always the last person to come back, and usually show up with the sweepers, who go through the trail to clean it up, because they're too tired to make it back on their own.

By the time they're back, everyone else is gone but me and a few others, who have to stay, and all of the supplies are put away, so they just get some water and a medal because we'd feel guilty if we didn't give one to them. They thank us for a great race, say they had a great time, and occasionally complain about the cut off all while we wait for them to finally leave.

I just nod, because that's what you do with crazy people.

THOUGHTS

3/2/17

I can't think of anything to write.

3/3/17

My mind isn't working today either.

3/4/17

This sucks so much.

[The rest of the page is covered in scribbles]

THE PROBLEM WITH GOOD AND EVIL

When we all imagine good and evil, different images pop into our heads. Maybe you see the Joker, or Hitler, or the average white male. No matter who you see, I want you to think about them, and decide with absolute certainty if that person is truly 100% evil. You probably decided yes, and that, is a problem.

If you look at good and evil from an unbiased point of view, which is impossible, you'll see that its two sides of the same coin. A coin that, in this case, looks exactly the same on each side. Without any opinion, good and evil can not be differentiated from each other, because they are not specific defined things.

Look at it this way, if you put a picture of Batman and a picture of the Joker, who both look equally intimidating, in front of a newborn baby and told it to point at which one was evil, there's a 50/50 chance as to who it's going to pick, because it doesn't have any previous views to use to choose an answer.

This is the reason why it's so hard to change someone's idea on what's good and evil. It's the same reason why so many people can't take criticism! Because they truly believe that what they are seeing or doing is good, and that we as people must be the evil ones for trying to claim that it isn't. *You* may think it's obvious that someone who hates gay marriage is hateful, but *they* believe that a truly good higher power doesn't like it, so *they* think that their actions are preserving those beliefs.

That's why it's so hard to change someone's views, because the argument of "It's evil!" doesn't hold any weight for someone who believes it's good. The majority of the world think that they're the people who are right, which is impossible since everyone's opinions contradicts someone else's, leaving us with a majority that has no moral high ground whatsoever, since they're all just on the same level, trying to convince themselves that they're taller than the person next to them.

It's only the minority who see themselves as evil who are truly despicable or undeniably good, and they can't even see that because if they did they'd be on the same level as everyone else. Some people like to claim they're in a "middle area" where they do enough good and evil to cancel itself out. But being good today doesn't make up for being bad yesterday, it's just something different.

This problem where we see someone's opinions as worse than our own will always exist because it's human nature, and so as time goes on it's likely that more arguments will end in screaming rather than mutual understanding. We'll always see good and evil differently from each other, and no matter how much we try people's opinions on us will not all be good or bad, they just will be. Look at yourself, right now you're reading this, and maybe one day, through a series of events that couldn't possibly be determined, you go down as the worst person in history.

But you wouldn't be wrong if you said you acted with good intentions.

THOUGHTS

1/5/17

You know what's the worst thing about stories? Villains who are just evil for the sake of being evil. Like, that's not smart storytelling, it just just makes everything less interesting and kinda destroys the purpose of villains in the first place.

Both heroes and villains need to be relatable people at times so we can not only see ourselves in their situation, but also we can learn what *not* to do as human beings.

Like, when was the last time you [scribbled out words] met someone who just hated the whole world for no reason? Never? Yeah, me too. Because those people don't exist. And so they shouldn't be in our literature, except when used to parody their use elsewhere.

Also give females more character development. Just, in general.

YOU, YOU, AND THE UNIVERSE

Sometimes, when I can't sleep, I think about all the mistakes I, and anyone else, has ever done. Why did I not study for that history test? Why did my teacher ignore my question? Why was Varric Tethras not a romance option in 'Dragon Age: Inquisition'? This, is pointless, usually, so when I decided to stop feeling terrible, I try to think about something else.

The infinite universe.

Because if the universe does go on forever, that means at some point it's going to repeat, and then repeat again, and then again an infinite amount of times. That means somewhere out there is another Earth, with another "me" and another "you," exactly like this one.

But there's also another "you" that didn't embarrass themselves in front of their friends that one time, or trip down the stairs, or throw up in gym class.

I think that's comforting. Sure there's an infinite amount of "Jakes" that are just as bad or worse than me, but there's also infinite ones that are better. There's plenty of "Jakes" who grew up to be famous, and others who have their own family, and more that are just starting their lives and have the chance to choose what they want to be again. Somewhere thousands and thousands of lightyears away, there's a "me" out there who isn't depressed, or anti-social, or nervous.

And if he got to that point, then why can't I?

THOUGHTS

Some of the best things I've ever heard:

Star, who has never played the clarinet: "I've been playing the clarinet for eight years, so, eat that."

———

Teacher 1: "I'm going to learn to shut up."

Teacher 2: "No you're not!"

———

[Churro is holding up Jam's bracelet that is made out of green balloons]

Churro: "It looks like a butthole."

Jam: "Stop!"

Me: "It's Shrek's butthole!"

[Jam screams]

———

[Star is eating a granola bar]

Star: "I'm a nasty human being."

———

[I put me foot against the wall, directly next to Clam's face. She screams]

Thor: "Are you okay? It was just a foot."

Clam: "No there was a leg too!"

Churro: "All my friends are cunts."

Me: "Does that mean I'm a cunt?"

Churro: "No not you you stupid fucking cunt!"

[After giving a two minute long speech about saxophones and then proceeding to pour out 5 year old canned lasagna into a cauldron burning over a fire]

Her: "This is terrible. I take back everything I ever said."

[During a heated discussion while we ate lunch]

Star: "You knowing nothing of the frisbee specialist. I had a one on one with a frisbee specialist."

Celery: "Who wants to be that? Who wakes up and is like, 'Oh yeah! That's what I want to be, a frisbee specialist'!"

Star: "Ultimate frisbee is my passion!"

TOOTH TROUBLE

My family has a long history of mouth problems, at least, on my father's side. And I'm not sure why, but while my brother was born with a normal, healthy mouth, I was born with a fucked up one.

It all started with how I spoke. Unlike everyone else I knew, I wasn't able to pronounce the "th" in normal words. Instead, it would come out like an "s." When you're a child, every lesson in school turns into a speaking contest, since that was something new that we were still trying to wrap our heads around. So, when you can't speak properly, you, as well as everyone around you, tend to get pretty frustrated.

Here's a fun list of words I used to pronounce incorrectly, just in case you want to know how it feels to be a kid with a speech impediment:

- This = sis (suh-is)
- Thunder = sunder (sun-der)
- Through = srough (suh-roo)
- These = sese (see-se)

- The = see (see)
- Thoughts = soughts (suh-ought-s)
- Think = sink (sink)

Now read this next sentence out loud while replacing the bolded words with the ones above: ***This thunder*** *I see* ***through these*** *windows ruins* ***the thoughts*** *I* ***think***.

Make you feel like an idiot, doesn't it?

Even back then I felt like I was stupid, because my teachers just didn't know how to deal with a kid who couldn't even pronounce *the* correctly. So we went to a special teacher, who after going through a few exercises with me had me lift up my tongue so she could look at my lingual frenulum. The lingual frenulum being the thin "skin web" holding your tongue down onto the lower jaw. She then told my parents to visit a doctor instead of her.

As it turned out, I was tongue tied, a.k.a. I had ankyloglossia, meaning my lingual frenulum was too short, and therefore, restricting my tongue movement. Depending on the severity, this can go away with time or even become ignorable after going through speech therapy, but the Martinez family doesn't have any time for that, so instead we went with the final option. Surgery. Specifically, lingual frenectomy.

Lingual frenectomy is when they cut the lingual frenulum to allow the tongue to move more freely, and if cutting the inside of your mouth sounds painful, that's because it is. Luckily for you, the surgeons can put you to sleep while they stick various sharp objects in your mouth. Unluckily for me, my father was scared that something would go wrong if I was asleep, so he made sure that they kept me awake the entire time.

Yes, my mouth was numbed, but I could still *feel* everything moving around the whole time. The surgery took an hour, and the whole time I kept my eyes shut because I was trying to imagine a situation where you were hurt but couldn't feel pain *other* than during a surgery or slow death. I did open my eyes for a few second about halfway through, but that was a bad idea because everything seemed more like an autopsy room than a children's hospital.

When the surgery was finally complete, I was given a bag of gauze to put in my mouth until the bleeding stopped, and then I was rushed home by my father who didn't even let me stay long enough to grab a sticker.

I wasn't allowed to eat anything solid for the next few weeks, so instead my mother had bought a massive amount of pudding and took out our old blender to make milkshakes. However, when I put the spoon in my mouth, every nerve in my body shout out in pain. I drank from a straw for two days, until my mother decided that I was being a little baby and refused to give me anything but a spoon.

Every bite I took made me burst into tears.

A few years later, my orthodontist noticed I had an overbite, and that in order to remedy this, I needed braces. At this point, unlike most children, I actually enjoyed going to the dentist. That was mostly due to me going to one of those fancy dentist offices with TVs over every chair and Playstation 2s with Jimmy Neutron games in the waiting room, but also partially due to the fact that I knew *real* mouth pain and so teeth cleaning didn't really phase me.

This all changed when I got my braces put in. They only went across my two front teeth, for some reason, but the pain my mouth felt every time they would tighten them felt just as terrible as it would have otherwise. Though, in my opinion, the worst part was actually when you would get the mold of your mouth created. There's just something about pink slime being stuck in your open mouth so forcefully that it not only hurts, but make it hard to breath, that I just didn't like.

My time with these braces were short lived, since two years later, they were removed, leaving my teeth feeling as if they were melting out of my mouth, which if you've had braces, you'll know that it feels surprisingly good. I spent the next few hours rubbing my tongue against my teeth, enjoying how smooth they were.

Unfortunately for me, while removing my braces, the orthodontist noticed a new problem. There was something wrong with my gums. I'm not sure on the details, which thankfully means that I don't have to look up medical mumbo jumbo, and you don't have to pretend you understand what it means. But basically, if I didn't get surgery, *again*, I would develop gum disease when I was around 15 years old. I sincerely hope I don't need to explain what gum disease is.

This time around, the surgery was easier to manage, for the most part. I was still awake, and it still was very uncomfortable to feel needles in your mouth without there being any pain, but I was used to it by now, and so despite the surgery being longer, it felt much quicker. Plus the surgeon was *very* talkative this time around.

The recovery was also easier, mostly because it was my gums and you don't have to put food on your gums to eat, so after the bleeding stopped I felt as good as ever before. My mouth troubles were finally over. But what's that? There's more paragraphs left to read? Well that because, as you probably assumed, there's still more to come.

During the summer before 6th grade, I was told that I, once again, needed braces. But they weren't just on my two front teeth this time, instead, they covered my whole mouth. If you've ever had braces that cover every tooth you have, then you'll know that it's really hard to keep food out of them, and so instead of focusing all your energy to keep them clean, it's a lot easier to just not smile ever again. And so I didn't smile for years, at least, not while showing my teeth.

In 7th grade, it only got worse, since now they had to drill some hooks into my gums so I could put some rubber bands across my mouth. I'm not sure why this is something that you have to do, but it was so difficult putting them in that for months I didn't even wear them. When I finally did start putting them in, it was only because my dad was willing to help me with it. And that is very embarrassing when you're in a dentist office.

After they were gone and my teeth stopped feeling like putty, I was given my very own retainer, complete with green box and easily bendable metal. Unlike everyone else I knew, I actually wore my retainer every day, for every hour of that day, because I was terrified of the idea of getting braces put back on my teeth.

I don't even think the orthodontist realized this, because instead of checking on my teeth like you're supposed to, he just assumed I didn't use it and kept having me wear it all day long. Since I'm nervous every single second of my life, I had to wait until my dad asked him about, and then, after two years, I was allowed to only wear my retainer when I went to sleep.

I no longer wear my retainer.

To anyone who has or is currently dealing with braces, or a speech impediment, or anything that's similar, I want you to know that you don't look or sound like an idiot, no matter how much you may think, and anyone who says you do is just asshole who should focus more on why no one likes them instead of what goes on behind your lips. I would offer other advice to people who may have a rotting tooth or cavity, but I don't think I properly can because I just don't know what it's like.

Despite how fucked up my mouth is, I've never had one.

THOUGHTS

9/19/17

I think that, now that I'm legally an adult, I know what I want my funeral to be like.

That sounds super dark but it's not.

I think I want people to be happy at my funeral. Happy sad. Sad happy. Because the whole idea of people crying over me just seems wrong in my mind. I want there to be a video of me reading my own will, complete with jokes and a dance section. Plus everyone has to wear colorful clothes the whole time.

I want my ashes to be split up evenly so everyone gets the same amount, and then that way they can place me wherever they think I'd want to be, and it wouldn't matter what I thought cause I'd be dead, and they could also hold onto me for as long as they want to before they let go. I don't know, I think it'd make it bittersweet and beautiful in a way.

SOOTHING SORES

When I was younger, and still had enough energy to move fairly regularly, I played tennis. Every wednesday, from 4:00pm to 5:30pm, I would take lessons with a very nice guy, and he would help me improve my endurance, speed, and overall skill. I wouldn't consider myself very good, especially since I didn't practice very consistently, but I still agreed to go to multiple weeks worth of tennis camps every summer.

These camps were hell.

They went from 8:00am to 5:00pm, usually during heat waves, and we got only two short breaks a day. Until lunch, we would switch around our group's teachers until we had spent time with every single one, and then after lunch we would do full length matches with other kids until we got to leave. It was slightly worse for me since not only was I unathletic by nature, but my partner in doubles also never did anything, so I had to work extra hard.

The next day, my legs would always be sore, and just moving them felt strange. Suddenly, every muscle I moved, I noticed, as if my body was constantly reminding me what I was doing every second.

It was, weirdly, nice.

I doubt I'll ever work out enough to get sore like that again in my entire life, but just remembering it makes me smile. It was like a reminder, that not only was my body working, but it would continue to, even with the weird feeling that was trying to get it to stop. I like to think of it as if it was someone you could learn from. They keep going and going until continuing hurts, so they take a second for it to stop, and then move forward.

And all that's left is the reminder that the worse has passed.

THOUGHTS

(Sometime before 5/2/16 but after 4/20/16)

I deal with over supination, meaning my feet turn more outward at the ankle then they're supposed to, and it's just kinda something I've always lived with.

It's weird because feet don't do that. They shouldn't do that. But mine do.

Plus to add even more onto that, I do weird stuff with my feet. Like sit on them all the time, even on chairs during class. I'm literally doing it right now. It leaves bruises and marks that probably aren't good but when I sit normally my legs start to tingle (is that the right word for it?) and then shake and then I have to move them into a weird position.

It sucks and I hate it, but honestly, everyone I know thinks it's kinda interesting because of how I sit, so even though I'll probably deal with serious leg injuries in the future, I'm going to keep doing it.

Plus if I stopped my legs would just start to tingle.

CHEWING ASPIRIN

Today's date is June 20th, 2017, and I feel like I'm dying. I'm not, which is good, but it would be better if my sinuses would clear up and my head would stop pounding faster than my heart. Being sick is horrible, I think we can all agree on that, and I would never wish any illness, even something as trivial as a cold, on anyone. Unless, of course, it meant that the next math test would be pushed back.

The interesting thing about being sick, or even in pain, is that once it's all over, we forget how it felt. So, a few years ago, I started writing down how I feel during these times of suffering in case it was ever necessary for me to remember. So far there hasn't been a life or death situation where I'd need to, but it is nice to look back on my previous feelings of pain and overall grossness.

One of my earliest memories of being sick was when my family and I were staying in a log cabin somewhere in the United States. It was the first time I had ever seen snow, and I wanted to enjoy it completely, but instead I had a high fever and an unstoppable appetite for saltine crackers.

I didn't eat anything but those crackers for two whole days because my stomach felt so bad, and in the middle of the night on the second day, I started throwing up. I spent the next 3 hours sitting next to the toilet with my mom, throwing up every time we thought it had finally stopped, and drinking 7-UP to soothe my stomach when we realized it hadn't.

If you're wondering why I didn't take some pills or even aspirin to stop the pain and symptoms, it's simply because I couldn't swallow them. Not because I would throw them up or my throat was in too much pain to, I just couldn't. For years I would have to get over any illness with sheer willpower, or chew my aspirin when I wanted to get rid of a headache. And, in case you were wondering, no. Aspirin does not taste good. It tastes like crushed up dirt mixed with baking powder and raw, unforgivable spite.

Now, this inability to swallow has led to a few bad instances in my very short life. For example, my parents like to remind me that when I was two years old, I had to take medicine that came in both pill form, and in the form of a suppository. I always went with the latter, since swallowing pills was out of the question, and because of this I usually tried to hide the fact that I was sick, which is not easy when you aren't even smart enough to count to ten.

For anyone wondering what a suppository is and why it's so bad, I'll tell you. It's similar to taking a pill, where you swallow it and then it dissolves in your stomach, only instead of putting it in your mouth, you put it up your ass. This, is not fun, and it often caused a great amount of tears to fall from my eyes and a lot of joy filled yells from my brother, who practically lived off my suffering.

Some years later, after I stopped needing medicine that had to go up my butt, I stayed for dinner at a friends house who, conveniently, had doctors as parents that carried around top tier medicine in case an emergency popped up. In this case, the emergency was my terrible stomach ache, and I was quickly handed a large clear pill that would apparently cure it instantly.

Maybe it would have, and maybe it wouldn't have, but I don't know, because I didn't take the pill. I did try to, multiple times in fact, but after four cups of water had been poured down my throat, I ended up spitting it out into the sink, making what must have been the strangest looking mess to clean up.

Despite these occasional incidents, I lived without severe sickness for most of my life. That is, until the 8th grade, when I suddenly had a crazy high fever that wouldn't go away. I spent an entire week laying on my couch, barely able to get enough strength to even eat before my father finally took me to the hospital. After about an hour of sitting, they checked my lungs and realized that no, I didn't have a fever, I had pneumonia, which is when you get a virus in your lungs that makes it difficult to breathe, causing the death of around

50,000 people a year in the United States.

The doctors gave me a few antibiotics afterwards, told me I would be fine, and after taking the medicine for a few days I felt as if none of it had ever happened.

Until, of course, it happened again.

One late saturday night after a band competition, my friend Thor and I were walking to our chaperone's car in the pouring rain. Thor, being the genius that he is, decided that it would be a great idea to take off his jacket and then encourage me to do the same. After a few *no*'s and even more *come on*'s in response, I gave in. After all there's nothing better than doing stupid stuff with your friends.

The next day I woke up too sick to move, and Thor woke up completely fine. As someone who has now had pneumonia twice, and has recorded how it feels, I think I can accurately sum up the next week of my life that followed. I was either sleeping, trying to actually breathe in enough air so I could move, or laying down on the couch as "The Mickey Mouse Clubhouse" played on TV. I felt like a tire that someone had popped and then continued to drive with for the next few hours. Drained, doomed, and disgusting.

The doctors once again gave me antibiotics to take for a few days, and after that, I was completely fine again.

I'm not sure how I learned to swallow pills, but one day, I just did. Gone were my days of sleeping through aches and chewing aspirin, now I could finally get as healthy as the rest of the human race. Or so I thought.

As it turned out, the only pills I had to swallow were ones for my acne and eventual acid reflux, but everything else had medicine in liquid form. I didn't even stop chewing aspirin, I just kept doing it, as if it was one last bit of pain before it kicked in and stopped my body from feeling like it got hit by a truck.

But even with aspirin, some things only go away with time, so I'll just have to wait out whatever my body seems to be doing to itself, because right now there's two pillows behind my head, three violent coughs from my lungs, and one more horrible day until it's all over.

Well, hopefully.

THOUGHTS

(Sometime in 2012)

I feel like shit. Like I'm coughing my throat out of my throat into a trash bag, but there's no serious pain except for some fucking annoying throat burning.

(Early 2014)

I'm too tired to move my body, so I'm writing this while laying down which is way too fucking [unintelligible handwriting] I can't even really sleep and all that plays on TV is kids shows and stuff that people think moms enjoy seeing. I want [can't read this part either].

(Unknown date)

My legs hurt so much and I don't know why it's like they're being crushed by an elephant and I already took aspirin but it hasn't done anything yet and I really don't want to be in this pain anymore so i'm trying to keep my mind on it and am also sitting on it to get rid of the pain but the pressure isn't helping I don't think.

9/7/17

Acid reflux makes my stomach feel terrible every three seconds, causes my throat to make weird sounds, and also causes unwanted almost vomit. It gives me heartburn and I am too young to have to deal with that. I need to go to the hospital.

DOGS WITH DIABETES

I'm not sure what it is about dogs, but if you're a child, that's almost always the pet you want. My family used to have a Golden Retriever named Doug, who was as large as he was kind. We loved Doug, and Doug loved us. He had been around since before I was born, and because of that, we grew a special connection that only two small brained creatures can have with one another. We would run around together, I would sneak him bits of my food, and sometimes he would lie down on the pillow next to mine, so in the morning he and I could start our day together.

I'll never know when Doug died, since as it turns out, he was never our dog to begin with. He belonged to another married couple, who weren't able to take care of him for a long time due to the husband being sick. When he finally got better, they brought their truck down to our house, had Doug jump in the back, and I never saw him again. The only reminder that he even existed in the first place is a small framed picture next to my bed, where the second pillow would be.

My brother and I begged for a new dog for years, hoping that one day our parents would give in and get one. They had the same generic reasons why we couldn't, with their only exception being my brother's allergy to animal fur. Of course, this detail didn't stop us from endlessly begging, and so one fateful day, my father took me to the pet store, and let me pick out a fish.

Its name, was Swimy. And we became the best of friends.

Despite the plastic walls keeping us apart, Swimy and I played tons of games. I'd drop his food in random places and he'd swim around quickly to catch it, he'd make bubbles and I'd count how many popped, or, we'd play my favorite game, hide and seek. I'd hide behind my bed, or in my closet, and after about a minute I'd claim that Swimy had found me and try to find him. I'd always pretend I didn't see him, after all, it wasn't his fault there weren't any good hiding spaces inside his tank.

Eventually, my mother must have grown envious of the deep personal connection me and Swimy shared, so she quietly took him to the sink, murdered him, and tried to play it off like an accident. She claims she "placed him in the wrong type of water," and the police may have bought that story, but I know the truth.

After I moved on from my grief, my parents bought us a large snake, and an even bigger enclosure to put it in. I don't remember its name, but I do remember there were a surprising amount of people who wanted it to be named Jake, so we'll call him that.

There isn't much to say about Jake the Snake. He ate mice, drank water, tried to escape his home, and just about everything else pet snakes like to do. The one time he actually did escape, it took us two days to find him behind an old shelf, cleverly curled in on himself until he was as small as he could possibly be.

No one really liked Jake, which is a shame, but understandable. Since he wasn't able to hold me or my brother's interests, my parents sold him to someone else, and despite hearing a few updates on how he was doing, I never cared enough to remember them.

After a few more years of begging for a dog, my dad went out to the pet store and came back with a Border Terrier, since they don't shed much, and named him King Edward the 7th, Eddie for short. He was tiny, still is, and was born with a mutated tail. Instead of it being long and curly like it was supposed to be, it was short and straight. We call it his stinger.

The first day we got him, my brother and I spent hours in the backyard running and jumping around him as he stayed surprisingly quiet. Due to my low stamina and overall fitness, I got tired quickly, and spent a decently large chunk of time watching my brother play outside while I drank a glass of lemonade inside our house.

I realized then that an actual dog was a lot different from what I wanted.

Years with Eddie went by smoothly. My brother and I neglected our dog duties, except for walking, and happily sat around while he broke his squeaky toys outside. Almost everything about him stayed exactly the same. He didn't grow bigger, he didn't get louder, and he only started getting gray hairs recently.

Of course, there were a few exceptions. Whenever he got shaved he looked like a chihuahua, and whenever his hair got too long he looked like a wookie. He got more aggressive to other dogs, but stayed calm around humans, and if the dog was small enough he would hold back his bark. For one week he ate my crayons, and the following week every piece of poop I was forced to pick up looked like chocolate ice cream mixed together with rainbow sherbet, though I have to say, it may have smelled even worse than usual.

About a year ago, Eddie stopped eating and started to hate walks.

Now if this was me we were talking about, this wouldn't seem that strange, but when it's a dog, you know something is wrong. Both of my parents shrugged it off, saying that he was just getting picky with his dog food because we spoil him, and that he was getting lazy because he was old. I asked my parents multiple times to bring my dog to the vet, but they didn't. At least, not until he collapsed, forcing my parents to not only miss the Seinfeld show they had bought tickets for, but to also finally admit that *yes, something is very wrong.*

The only problem was, the vets couldn't figure out what that was.

It took months and thousands of dollars for the vets to conclude that Eddie had diabetes. So, my father and I drove to walmart, got a month's supply worth of animal insulin, and started giving my dog a shot every single day. Seeing an animal get a shot looks far more hopeless than a person getting one, and so I was lucky that my parents didn't make me give him one every day.

After a month had passed, we went back to the vet to see if there were any changes inside his body, since his behavior hadn't been affected at all. And, as it turned out, there was a pretty big change. Eddie wasn't diabetic any more. In fact, *he wasn't diabetic in the first place.* This was the last straw that made my parents give up on the vets.

It took a few weeks, but we found someone else who may have been able to help. She was a vet, yes, but also a hippie who worked without anyone controlling her, besides the law. The first thing she did was check Eddie's thyroid gland, because as she explained, it was one of the most simple causes for problems in dogs, so simple that it sometimes gets overlooked because it seems too obvious. And wouldn't you know it, Eddie doesn't *have* a thyroid gland.

After all of this was sorted, Eddie was finally able to improve. He's still slow, old, and picky, but he does eat, and only occasionally throws it back up anymore. The only problem is that now, he has dementia, making him forget where the dog door is and, therefore, shit all over the house.

And it doesn't look like rainbow sherbet this time.

THOUGHTS

3/1/17

Walking Eddie is so strange now. First of all, I rarely have to do it now, and second, we travel half the distance and it takes the same amount of time because he is unbelievably slow. I swear to god, the stuffed animal dogs I used to make lego bones for could walk faster.

Plus everyone with a dog wants to talk to me, since he's the size of a puppy, but he has gray hair. It's so uncomfortable for me because talking sucks, especially to strangers, and so I'm glad my dog hates other dogs because it allows me to leave the conversation early and not feel bad about it.

5/14/17

I don't know why but I just remembered all the times Eddie peed where he wasn't supposed to.

[Drawing of pee puddle, done in highlighter]

The first was when he peed in my dad's car. Only I didn't want to get him in trouble so I cleaned it up with a scholastic book list when he wasn't looking, and then rushed him to the backyard when the car was parked.

The second was when he peed on my foot in the middle of the kitchen. Directly on it. He literally stood over my foot and decided that that would be a good place to pee.

[Drawing of foot, with highlighter pee falling on it]

PIT

When I began my freshman year of high school, a surprising amount of my friends wanted me to join the marching band. I despised this idea. I'm not sure *why* I hated it so much, but everything about it seemed like something I wouldn't enjoy. There was a huge amount of time you had to commit to practicing and shows, plus I had no idea how to play an instrument or read sheet music.

And then I joined them at a football game.

My friends Thor, a girl we'll call Watson, another girl we'll call Liberty, and yet another girl we'll call Gingerbread, all forced me into Liberty's car on a friday night, and drove me to a school our football team was playing against. I wore Liberty's school jacket to pass as a band member and get in for free, and then we all headed up to the bleachers to watch the game.

I loved it. Not because I liked watching sports, which I don't, and not because I enjoyed the music, which I did, but because I got to spend time being an idiot with my friends. We joked, and ran, and hit tambourines all while talking to each other about anything we wanted to know. For example, while Watson, Thor, and I went to get a drink from the concessions stand, Thor explained that people thought me and him were dating, which was weird since only one of us was gay while the other had a girlfriend. Watson then turned to me, looked very surprised and gasped, *You have a girlfriend?*

I died laughing.

After that night, I agreed to join the marching band, with the only problem being that we were two weeks into the school year and they couldn't accept anyone else. But Pit could. In case you don't know what Pit is, it's the front ensemble, a.k.a. the musicians at the front of a marching band who don't march because their instruments are too large.

Since I didn't need to learn the marching routine, only the music, I was welcomed in and given the task of playing the bongos and symbol. Singular symbol. I hit it with a stick.

Everyone in Pit accepted me right away, and I quickly got to know all of them. There was Heart, C1, C2, Brownie, Bread, Muscle, Mini, and Cerberus. We were all instructed by Zelda, and also had an honorary member named Beef. To give you a better idea of who they are, I'll tell you what it was like to play with them.

Heart was, and still is, absolutely amazing. She's smart, talented, and one of the few members who I still talk to today. I spent the most amount of time with her, talking and playing music, and we all felt a little lost without her when she travelled to China for two weeks and couldn't make it to a few of the shows. Out of everyone, she was the kindest.

C1 was a bit of a different story. She was also kind and accepting, and near the beginning I talked with her the most, but she was also controlling and started drama that didn't need to be started. I won't forget the stupid song names we made together, but unfortunately, I don't think our 'Lumberjack' album is ever going to release.

C2 shares the same name as C1, but he couldn't be more different. He was quiet and reserved, but still hilarious and likable. I spent a lot of time with him just trying to make jokes, and I don't think Pit would have been as fun without him.

Brownie was mostly boring, with a few bits of dry humor thrown in every once in awhile, but we mostly just got along because he gave everyone free junk food.

Bread was the student leader of Pit, and was even more bland and boring than Brownie was. He got mad easily, focused only on the task at hand, and never looked at anyone without glaring. I will give him some credit though, he did keep us all in check.

Muscle and Mini were practically the same person. They never wanted to play what they were told to or talk to anyone but each other, and if it weren't for the fact that I was next to them the whole time and had to switch places with Muscle on the bongos during the second act, I probably would have forgotten they existed.

Cerberus was actually 3 separate girls, but they acted so alike and spent so much time together that they might as well have been one person. They talked a lot about anime, and video games, and always acted like mother figures to the rest of the group. I only have fond memories of them, but it's more of a parental type of fondness rather than a friendly one.

Zelda was slightly less strict than Bread, despite being the adult, and wrote all of our music as well as instructed us during most of our lessons. She ended up doing a lot of rewrites though, since she tended to accidentally put in video game music rather than something original.

Finally, Beef, the honorary member of our group. She always talked with Heart and I, and she still does, all while being a member of the actual marching band. I got on her nerves most of the time, but despite that, we became pretty good friends and found ourselves enjoying the constant bickering we always got into.

These people became my friends and bandmates for the rest of that year, and because of them, Pit became this weird family that always had to stick together since most of the actual marching band enjoyed ignoring us.

My first time playing with the band was during open house. Everyone stood out in the grass for an hour and played while Pit hit some tambourines because we didn't want to take out our equipment. It was stupid, and I loved it. Afterwards I bought a sweater with very tight arms that had the vanguard logo on it, and all my friends and I locked ourselves in one of the practice room where we screamed and did our best to change catchy tunes into Sex Ed propaganda.

Our real shows were, surprisingly, very similar to the ones where we goofed off on the tambourine. Sure, it was now a competition and we had to play real songs after having to push all our instruments to the front of the field and set up in under a minute, but other than that, we just hung out.

We didn't do very well that year, so instead of worrying about our placement at the end of each competition, we all just ate food on the bleachers and laughed as every other band went out and did it all perfectly. Then at the end of the day, we got on a bus, and went home. It was uneventful, which allowed it to be both freeing and enjoyable the whole way through.

At one of our random shows, I got our friend Bleach's number, and proceed to send him pictures of himself along with the creepiest texts a freshman could think of. I even changed my number in my phone, that way when he asked me to show him my number, it was something completely different. The conversation went like this:

[Picture of Bleach] Hello. Bleach.

"Wtf"

[Picture of Bleach's back] You can't run Bleach.

"Um"

"Jake"

Sorry. Not a "Jake."

[New photo of Bleach] And even if I was you couldn't hide.

"K"

"Then who"

Maybe I'm you.

[Photo from Bleach's facebook] You can't escape me Bleach.

"You're not me youdumb. Ass"

"Ok"

"..........."

What, Bleach, are you at a

[Picture of Bleach's face] Loss of words?

He found out it was me right after that, and pretty much stayed mad at me for years. In fact, every time he looked at me he would frown and ignore everything I said, until my Junior year, when he decided that he didn't need to anymore. I never texted Bleach again, and I'm pretty sure that even if I tried it would just tell me that I was blocked.

At another competition, which I had to leave early because I was sick, my parents tried to get there in time to see us perform, but due to the insane amount of traffic at the school, they showed up the second we finished. They never got to see me perform, in fact, none of my family did, because at the homecoming game, which my brother watched, the rest of the marching band didn't give Pit any time to set up, so none of us got to play.

During the yearbook photo shoot for band, I expected everyone from Pit to be there, but that wasn't the case. Only C2, Heart, and I showed up, and since we were the only Pit members there, we decided that we must be the best. We named ourselves "Best of Pit," took tons of photos together, and excluded any other members from joining. It was a very exclusive group.

A few months after football season, and therefore marching band season, had ended, my friends told me that if I payed $20, I could come with them on the yearly Disneyland trip. It was the best spent $20 of my life.

After a two hour bus ride filled with songs, games, and screaming, we all arrived at Disneyland and were taken backstage to prepare for our show in the parade. We were all told to not take pictures or videos because that would "ruin the magic," and so I didn't. They never said anything about describing it though, so I'll do that instead.

Disneyland, behind the scenes, is a dump. The buildings look like factories, there's trash everywhere, and most of it smells like horse shit. While we got changed into our warm uniforms in the 100 degree weather, I took the chance to try and spot everything terrible that I could. I saw Goofy smoking, more workers smoking, and a lot of other people who looked like they'd rather die than be there. The only good thing I saw was a taco truck, which just made me mad because, in case you didn't know, they don't sell tacos at Disneyland.

After we marched, which went surprisingly well, we once again ended up behind the scenes, where we stood for two hours since we had to wait behind all the floats. By the time we had made it back into the park, we were all soaking wet and smelling terrible. We then proceeded to ruin every other guest's day since we couldn't shut up during the rides.

We finally left at 12:00 am, when the park closed, and waited in the parking lot for the bus to arrive. And waited. And waited. Until we finally found out that the bus company thought we were going to be picked up at 12:00 pm the next day. Disney was nice enough to let us sleep on one of the convention room floors for 5 hours until the bus finally arrived, meaning that when I finally walked back into my house, it was 7:00 am, and my parents just stared at me as I went upstairs to go to sleep.

That was the last time I ever hung out with all of Pit, and despite it being the last, and probably most chaotic, memory I have of them, it's not my favorite. Before our last show, Cerberus turned to all of us and said, *Okay, when we nod, we're all going to jam out, okay?* And despite the pressure of our last show, despite the tension between some of us, when Cerberus nodded, we all leaned back, bounced with our knees, and smiled after every note.

When we finished the set, and turned to face the rest of the band as they marched into formation, I couldn't help but cry.

THOUGHTS

Genes:

My grandfather grew up with an orange in his hand,
holes in his socks, and pennies under his feet,
while my grandmother was raised with her photos in the paper
and a fruit crown on her head.

My mother threw her food in the dirt,
while my father picked bullets from the ground.
At ten years old he took a plane ride from
Cuba to New York and never looked back.

After four failed marriages blocked their way,
my parents met, and together
their genes melded into a beautiful baby boy.
My brother.

Then a few years later,
while my mother was cruising up the 15th,
a radio host said their was no name cooler

than a name like Jake.

And so I was born.

I was raised on queen sized beds,
school house chairs, and dusty old plane seats.
My hands screamed artist,
But my heart yelled fireman

And to this day I still haven't found a proper in-between.

I love stories,
and I love to talk,
but those two don't always
go hand in hand.

So when my words spill from my mouth in mumbles
they land on a page made from my tears
and the creation is both unimaginably
beautiful and horrifically ugly.

But no matter how much I try
those words are more me than my genes

and so while I can't pass on those

I can pass on this:

My name is Jacob.

I had a grandpa named Dots,

and a grandma named Barb.

My father was an immigrant,

my mother is not.

My brother is perfect,

but my words are stringed in

spirals called genes.

and they make me,

Me.

BOMB THREAT BLUES

My elementary and middle school was small and quiet. Everyone knew each other, no one *really* liked everyone, though most put up a pretty good act, and we never had any emergencies at all. We'd always prepare for them of course, but throughout my whole 8 years spent at Grant K-8, the worst thing that happened was when my 3rd grade teacher burnt something in the microwave. Twice.

Point Loma High School, however, is a completely different story.

The first lockdown I ever experienced was during freshman year PE. My male friends and I, since the girls were moved into their own class, all sat around in the weight room doing the bare minimum amount of movement required in order for the teacher to give us credit. We were completely bored out of our minds, since at that point in the year the teacher started collecting phones before class started. We would have talked if it weren't for the fact that we were in each others classes, so we were already caught up on everything that had happened that day.

Then suddenly the bells around us started ringing and didn't stop, which could mean three different things. Either **A)** There's a bomb threat, **B)** There's a shooter, or **C)** There's both. Everyone was quickly pushed together into a straight line in front of the teacher as he told us to remain calm and follow his instructions.

Now, if you've never been in the Point Loma High School weight room before, lucky you, then you wouldn't understand how perfect our location was. Sure, the weight room is compact, occasionally loud, and always smells like warm saliva, but it also has only one real door, two huge metal roll up ones, and no windows that someone could shoot you through. It felt like a bunker, and in this situation, it was probably just as safe as one.

Our teacher knew as much as we did as to why the bell went off, so he calculated the dangers of every situation, and made the logical decision to move the large 40-something group of students out of the weight room and all the way across the football field. Which caused my friend's and I, as well as others, to endlessly repeat things like, *We're going to die*, *If a shooter sees us we're dead*, and *Why are we in the middle of the football field?*

Obviously, no one died, and we all made it to the big gym with only slight psychological trauma. Once there, we were greeted by three other PE classes who all quietly sat on the bleachers in their own separate corners, and as we took our own spot in the last corner remaining, we were met with the horrible realization that our phones were all still in the weight room.

Eventually, everyone got bored again, and we all sat around in silence while secretly hoping that the shooter would come and knock on our door or something. Then, someone knocked on the door, and the panic started again. For the next few horrifyingly long minutes, our teacher talked to the person on the other side of the door, before letting him in. As it turned out, the kid just went off campus to get some In-N-Out, and didn't actually want to kill us all, or at least, didn't try to.

A few minutes later, the principal announced that everyone was safe, and we all quickly shuffled outside.

It wasn't until the next day when I found out why the school went on lockdown.

Someone had sent a bomb threat a few hours earlier, and while yes, that is pretty serious, I'm not sure how much sense it makes to stay on school grounds when there's supposedly a bomb *on school grounds*. Then again, I'm not a bomb expert. Maybe if the person who threatened to kill people sees the people they are about to kill they'll gain a conscience? No. Probably not.

We didn't get another bomb threat until next year, while everyone was getting ready for lunch to be over so we could go to class. My friends and I were waving goodbye to the strange old woman across the street, and as we stood up before the bell rang, the alarm went off. We were all quickly pushed into the nearby spanish room by a random teacher, and once the door was closed behind us all the lights went out.

Now, there are three different types of teachers you can get when it comes to lockdowns. You either get a teacher who doesn't care and lets you play ping pong, a teacher who gives everyone baseball bats and hides, or a teacher who makes you stay in complete silence until everything is over. Sadly, our teacher fell into the silent category, and while surrounded by darkness we all looked at each other in as many ways possible in an attempt to talk without words.

As time passed, we all grew more and more bored, until finally we broke out into song. I'm not sure what it sounded like to the teacher, but when we all sang "All Star" in semi-harmony, there was nothing more beautiful.

We left a few minutes later, after being shushed a few times and an announcement confirmed that it was a false alarm. Another bomb threat. Figures.

A few months later, at the end of first period, the alarm went off again. The doors were locked, the windows were covered poorly, and we all started to talk loudly because this was nothing we hadn't seen before. To our teachers credit, she did tell us to be quiet, but when over 30 kids are all working against you, you tend to give in easily.

Second period passed, then third, and with those passing hours we all became more and more carefree. A few kids tried watching Scooby-Doo, the live action one, before giving up, and a few others tried actually doing their homework, but everyone else just got louder and louder. At one point a girl told us to be quiet, because what if a shooter heard us? But we all quickly shut her down, because we were on the complete opposite side of school, so why would a shooter target us when they could kill way more students near the school center?

Yes, my teacher agreed, *That's true, but don't start getting any ideas.*

Eventually, a police officer told us that it was just another bomb threat and that it would all be over soon, and the excitement died down as we all waited to be let out. After about 30 minutes a girl admitted that she had to use the bathroom desperately, so we all moved a cabinet in front of her, and handed over the emergency bucket. For the next 60 seconds, we all sang "Happy Birthday" so loud that no one could hear her, the ending of the song being mixed in with another bell that meant we were free to go.

And I've never heard anything more beautiful.

THOUGHTS

4/15/17

I just had an out of body experience in a Target parking lot.

I was with 3 of my buds, and we had just left IHOP at around 11 pm and were playing music as loud as we could in my friend's car while we waited for all the songs we queued up to finish. I'm not sure why, but halfway through 'Bohemian Rhapsody' I assumed that our car, and the two parked cars in front of us were suddenly moving forward, but in actuality the car to our left was just backing out.

Time felt so still, like the music was controlling everything and I don't think I'll ever be able to listen to that song the same way again.

[In poorly erased pencil at the bottom of the page: Mama, ooooooh~]

5/23/17

Wanna know something weird?

You know how every high school movie has the crazy party scene where everyone gets drunk and tears the house apart? Turns out, those actually happen.

Isn't that weird? I thought it was a myth for years, and it just turns out that nobody invites me to anything outside of school.

I just assumed everyone has their friends over and they play cards till 2 am like I do, or go to Target and screw around, but no.

Teenagers get drunk.

I probably shouldn't be surprised.

8/5/17

I just had a photo shoot in a Target parking lot.

I was in a shopping cart, my four friends were posing around me, I had pizza in my hand, and a random guy kept his headlights on for us since it was around 11:30 pm and we couldn't see anything.

Then all we bought was 3 things of glue and a Bratz doll.

I think I understand why I don't get invited to parties.

BOX OF SOCKS

My grandfather, who we called Dots, had a christmas tradition where he would wrap up 20 to 30 different boxes with various items in them, and then, whenever we visited him and my grandma, who we called Grammy, me and my brother would get to pick out and open one each. This was a very tough process since while some boxes had money in them, others had oranges and socks that were far too big for our feet, which were very difficult to differentiate when you couldn't see them.

I didn't understand the significance of every gift when I was 3 years old. I didn't understand that Dots had been poor, and unable to afford socks, or that every gift was something he wished we could have that he couldn't. But I was a little kid, and I wanted money, not socks, and so when I didn't get what I wanted, I made sure to show clear disappointment.

But Dots didn't only give me physical gifts, he passed down other things, like his blue eyes, or love for popcorn, or tendency to pick up coins off the street, or his weird habit when walking where one arm dangled and the other would go around his back and hold onto it. All of these things were passed down to me too, and whether it was through science or coincidence, I still ended up the same way.

Dots passed away due to cancer on August 29th, 2006, 18 days after his 77th birthday. I was 6 years old.

I was already told months in advance that it would happen, we all knew it would, and even then I wasn't quite sure what it was supposed to be like when someone died. Everyone was sad, should I have been sad? I didn't *know* Dots at all. He was this man who had given me everything he could but at that point all I knew were the gifts, not the person behind them.

Everything returned to normal after a few years, once all of the sock boxes had been opened and everything else he owned was moved into the garage. Grammy would smile, and kiss our cheeks, and make us eat vegetables promising that it *Tastes just like candy!* which it never did.

Eventually Grammy started seeing a new man, we'll call him Apple, who she finally married in 2016. He, is an interesting case. He's the same age as Grammy, and has a cat just like she does, and plays music that Grammy loves more than life itself. He's nice, just a bit stubborn, and always tries to get along with everyone and be interested in what they enjoy.

Apple wants to be a part of a family that still isn't ready to let him in. Everyone is still clinging tightly to Dots's memory so hard that no one is ready to let Apple fill in that spot for him. It's horrible, no matter what he does everyone finds something wrong with Apple, and I always just sit there wondering why they can't just help this loving man find a place he belongs.

Grammy is terrified of being alone, so she clings to Apple, and I think he clings back because he wants someone who cares about him just as much as he cares about them. And I love Apple, I know him better than I knew Dots, and maybe thats *why* I'm able to love him.

Apple is a person I know, but Dots is the man who keeps on giving. Even now, my grandmother gave me hundreds of pages of rewrites and new stories for the Canterbury Tales handwritten by himself. These papers hold so many bits and pieces of him in them, thousands and thousands of words that he would have said if he was here.

The Canterbury Tales captured my grandfather's mind in a way I'll probably never understand, but I'm inching forward with every page. And maybe that's enough, since at the bottom of the stack he wrote one more gift for me:

It's rough and lousy, but maybe Johnny or Jake may want to do something with it.

I will Dots.

I will.

THOUGHTS

12/25/16

It's interesting how different holiday stories and traditions seem when you're old enough to fully understand them. It's kinda like you're watching an old TV show now that you're older and getting all the sex jokes, rather than thinking back on who you were and what you were doing when you were younger.

Like, today's christmas, and it always makes me think back to when I thought Santa was real and that he somehow did travel the world super quickly and delivered every kid whose family earned moderate income gifts. And I can't understand how I believed it because not only did it not make any sense, but also every christmas movie I used to watch emphasized how unrealistic it was.

How did every adult not believe in Santa even though he was real? How does that happen? When did people stop believing in him and why? Also, who did they think the random new presents were coming from? You could argue that they thought the other parent bought it, but there is a zero percent chance that the parents wouldn't talk about how the other one bought them stuff without informing the first parent, and then they'd realize that neither of them bought it so that means that either Santa is real or Robin Hood is still alive.

There was also the tooth fairy, who I knew wasn't real because my mom wasn't subtle about leaving me cash, but she was creepier than everyone else because no one ever had a complete answer on what exactly she does with the teeth. Are there just jars of it somewhere?

The most interesting one to me though was the easter bunny, because my parents never even pretended he was real, but we would still hunt for easter eggs in my small backyard. It was just my brother and I and around 50 eggs, but we would spend hours searching for them. When I was 5 I thought that was because we had a million plastic eggs laying around, but it turns out that it's really because while we'd search, Dots would pick up the eggs from our baskets and place them around so we'd keep looking.

I can imagine him smiling, her legs cracking a little when he squats down to hide something behind a bush. And then I imagine his face lighting up when he'd see us open his presents on christmas, or how he'd give out more money than a tooth fairy would for a thousand teeth.

[Slight water damage]

I think I'm going to stop writing now.

JUST LIKE HIM

I was born roughly 3 years after my brother John. Although, to me, he was Johnny, since my Dad and my brother sharing the same name was too complicated for my tiny child brain to comprehend. I was given the name Jacob, in order to keep the same first letter as every other male in my immediate family, and also because my Mother heard it on the radio and thought it sounded cool.

At the ripe young age of one, my hair was still blindingly blond, and my blue eyes were an irregularity only me and my Grandfather shared. Like a lot of babies, I was fat, though some would argue that that made me even cuter as a child. I'm not sure which of these traits peaked my brother's interest, but when he returned from a baseball game later that day and saw me, he became obsessed.

I became this brand new thing for him, like an expensive toy straight off the shelf. He spent as much time with me as humanly possible, often watching me like a hawk for hours at a time. It's supposed to be practically impossible to look that far back, but when I close my eyes and think, I swear that I can see his young face looking down at me, his eyes filled to the brim with what must have been pure joy.

As I grew up, my brother became the center of my existence, and I stopped being the center of his. He was an idol, competitor, friend, genius. Everything he did was something I wished I could do. Everything involving academics came as second nature to my brother, but it didn't for me. While he picked up on sports, music, math, science, art, literature, complex human interactions, and anything else you can think of, I sat behind him and watched silently, mindlessly smiling the entire time.

During this time I was far too forgiving. My brother would say something mean, take something of mine, or physically hurt me to the point where I would run away with tears pouring down my face, and an hour later, he would apologize, ask if we were still friends, and I would respond with the worst cliche any elementary school student could say. "We're not friends, we're brothers."

To my brother, this served as a sentimental act of forgiveness. To me, it served as a constant reminder that not only was I unable to come up with anything more than a laughably bad line from a low budget film, but I also wasn't able to tell my brother when to fuck off, and do something to make up for what he had done.

Despite the minor hardships, my view on my brother stayed unchanged. I wanted to help this incredible man with anything he could ever need, just to help repay him for all the good he had already done for the world. I became my brother's personal servant, or more accurately, slave, since at least servants get compensation.

I did simple tasks like get drinks for him, carry his 50 pound backpack, or sit still and be quiet for so long that I looked like a statue every single day. I never got more than a few half hearted thanks, but at that point, that's all I needed to survive.

Later on, one fateful day in July, my brother threw a football. This sounds like nothing, and it should have been, except the football wasn't thrown into someone else's arms, it was thrown into one of my carefully crafted lego structures. The brick building wasn't spectacular, or even slightly good, but I spent hours on it until it came out good enough for me to actually be proud of something *I* did.

Needless to say, the structure was completely destroyed, and enough pieces were lost so that it could not be rebuilt again. *This is okay*, I thought, slowly starting to grab the remains from the ground, *Johnny will apologize and everything will be fine*. Except he never did apologize, and while the moment was only a few minutes long, it was the first time when I saw my brother in a different light.

For years my views and the world's views were interlocked into one large structure. I felt guilty for not being as good as my brother, and so I tried to become him in every way. I grew my hair to my shoulders, wore the ugliest jackets you could find, and put on jeans every morning, before taking them off and deciding shorts were the best way to go. While doing homework, I would count each second till 20 minutes had passed, and then ask my brother for help so I could see exactly how he did it.

But in the 5th grade, the heat trapped from my hair must have burned through my skull because at that time I realized that I did not want to be like my brother at all. I cut my hair short, stopped wearing jackets, and threw every pair of jeans I owned away, even if I had never worn them. In those moments where the trash built up, my closet emptied, and hair fell from my head, I separated from the world, leaving behind a small hole that was quickly filled by the simplest of things.

Compared to my brother, I was no one. And for good reason. My brother was *still* absolutely perfect in every way. Looked perfect, acted perfectly, said the perfect things at the perfect times. Before he came out, everyone thought he had a beautiful girlfriend. And after he came out, he had a real, beautiful boyfriend. When I came out, the closest thing I had to a relationship was the one time a boy handed me a handful of rocks in the school's bathroom because they reminded him of me.

Johnny took control of every conversation, explaining every little detail of his plan for the rest of his life. He wanted to be a pharmacist, then start a nonprofit organization, then help the poor, then fly off to space and make contact with aliens. As far as the world was concerned, this was destined to happen, and so my brother received constant praise and firm shoulder grabs from those older than him. I was busy just being glad that no one wanted to ask me what I had planned, since at that point, I didn't have anything.

Before he left for college, my parents, Johnny, and I, were all driving home when my brother broke down into tears. For those few minutes, I saw my brother trapped like he's never been before. He was scared, worried about my parents opinion of him, and breaking down more and more because my mom just couldn't say the right words. I turned away from this scene, stared out the car window into the night, and guiltily smiled.

There's a kind of pain that comes with enjoying another's misfortune, the type that kills you inside by making you feel bad for being happy. You wonder if other people feel like this too sometimes, and then slowly shake your head no. People don't feel like this, monsters do. And of course I was a monster, who wouldn't be when compared to him.

The time apart gave me few chances to breathe, because despite Johnny being gone, his presence was always there. Now at every gathering, he was the topic of conversation. Everyone wanted to know what Johnny was doing. Are his grades good? *Yes*. Is he exceeding our expectations? *Yes*. Is he in a relationship? *Yes!* For the first time in years, I wanted my brother to come back so people would stop asking.

But when he did come back, people just asked more. Even I got caught back in the trap again. I found myself thinking back on how things used to be, wondering what went wrong and why, despite the answer always seemingly being nothing.

I searched through every corner of my phone in search of photos. My goal was to find something that had meaning to both of us. Something that could send him back off to college with the memory of us together, so maybe the mistake that was never made could finally be fixed. But I couldn't find anything. And so my brother leaned over and told me that if I didn't want to talk to them, I shouldn't have come.

When the time came for him to leave, I did not say goodbye.

I laid awake for hours that night, my feelings of envy mixing together with sadness into one emotional mess. I don't know when I finally fell asleep, but when I opened my eyes again, it was morning and my brother was gone. The sun shined through my windows, small gusts of wind slowly froze my arms solid, the sad sounds of my parents steps echoed throughout the house, and I smiled my guilty smile.

THOUGHTS

6/20/17

Wanna know the worst thing my mother has ever said to me? *Are you even trying?*

I'm not sure what it is about going on guilt trips that hurts so much, but the second you board that plane, you kinda realize that whoever bought you that ticket is completely despicable.

To be fair, sometimes people deserve to feel guilty. For example, did you cheat on your girlfriend, steal her cat, and then throw a rock through her window? If so, you deserve to feel like shit. But the thing is, I didn't do anything even remotely like that.

I was just failing Algebra II. Which, for the record, wasn't entirely my fault.

[Poorly erased next to "fault": 2 Cool + 2 Be = 4 Gotten]

I've never been good at math, at any point in my life, so in 6th grade when they put me in the regular math program rather than the advanced one, I was actually able to learn and keep up fairly well. It was my mother who called my school when she found out and demanded for me to be placed in the advanced class, which I am thankful for since I made most of my friends there, but it's clear to see that once I got to that point my math grades took a nosedive into oblivion.

I could never keep up in math, throughout all of middle school and clearly into high school, but it wasn't because I wasn't trying. I tried *so hard.* And you know what that does? When someone sends you on a guilt trip after years of trying your best?

It makes you stop trying.

#TEENFATGUYS

The movie *Click*, starring Adam Sandler, came out on June 23, 2006 to such amazing reviews such as: "This movie sucks!" (Lori Hoffman) and "[Click] is an abomination." (Joe Morgenstern). Despite the concept being bad and the execution being even worse, as a child, I really loved the movie, though I didn't know why for a couple years.

After seeing it a few times, I became more and more fascinated with the scene where he travels into the future and turns out to be very, very, fat. I used to stick a surprisingly sturdy beach ball under my shirt when I was alone, and spend a very long time rolling back and forth on it while trying to get plastic food into my mouth. This could all be grouped in with me being an over imaginative kid and clinging to anything I found vaguely interesting, but after the fascination didn't go away in the following years, I accepted that it had to be something that would always stay in the back of my mind for the rest of my life.

Resident Evil 6 came out in late 2012, and despite many people not liking it, I thought it was at least enjoyable. After playing through the entirety of Leon's campaign, I decided to move on to Chris Redfield's, where I quickly realized that I was spending a much longer amount of time in his story than in Leon's. I kept dying, and restarting, and making the same careless mistakes over and over again before I finally realized why I kept messing up.

I was distracted by Chris's ass, which just so happened to be in my line of vision the entire time playing.

Once I realized this I paused the game, and ran over to my iPad to start looking up a few things online. The first was an *Am I gay?* quiz, which had great questions such as: "Do you tackle him when playing football just so you're closer together?" which I couldn't relate to since I personally don't know the definition of exercise. The second was just *Chris Redfield*, where I spent an embarrassingly long amount of time scrolling through shirtless pictures of him, getting more and more confused since his abs weren't doing anything for me.

In the end, I accepted that I was gay, and decided that I would only look at pictures of Chris wearing a shirt from now on.

I came out in 8th grade, and like most people, it was to my friends first and my family second. The first person I ever told was Poise, who responded with a shocked gasp before saying, "I *knew* it, but I *didn't*," and then proceeding to tell my other friend Color less than five minutes later. All my other close friends found out in the coming months, both because of me and because of others.

The first family member I ever came out to was my mother, just a few weeks after I had come out to Poise. She had called me downstairs, I grabbed the salad she left me off the counter, and as I walked away, I turned to her, shrugged my shoulders, and said, "Hey mom? I'm gay." And then I went to my room.

After a few minutes, my mom came up into my room and whispered, *That's okay*. And I wanted to say, "Yeah Cynthia, I know it's okay, you don't need to remind me," but instead I just rolled my eyes and listened to her numerous questions where she tried to make me tell her that somebody was bullying me which, for the record, nobody was.

Later, she told my dad, who gave me the same talk, and after that nothing happened. I was honestly a little disappointed. I *at least* wanted a rainbow cake or card or something.

Now, if you knew my family, you'd know they are very accepting of everyone. *Not straight?* Doesn't matter. *Transgender?* That's cool. *Different race than us?* Sweet. Yet despite this acceptance, there were a few exceptions. For example, my mom makes very rude assumptions about everyone and then repeats those assumptions every couple of minutes until she finds someone else to pick on. Which, in case you didn't know, isn't very fun.

This, however, doesn't bother me much, since I can just tune it out and at least the people she's talking about will never know.

What does bother me isn't something about just my mother, though she is the biggest offender of it by far. It is instead, something my whole family is guilty of. They all *hate* fat people. I'm not even sure why, but every time we see, talk to, or walk by anyone who is even slightly overweight, I hear the same comments.

Jeff's sons are both interested in food eating contests now.

"Really?"

Yeah. They've both blown up but Jeff seems really proud of them.

"Ha! If we had a fat child, we'd hide them in the corner."

Absolutely disgusting.

"I can't believe they actually go outside like that."

I know! Isn't it so gross?

When they walk by, you can feel the whole room shaking.

There was a huge shirtless guy walking around outside.

"Huge as in strong or fat?"

Fat.

"Well I'm sure someone found him attractive."

Yeah, freaks maybe.

If you grow up hearing this like I did, you quickly start to realize that if you're fat, there's no place for you in the family. It's not like they're going to kick you out or anything, but they'll be talking about you behind your back, and it'll be pretty obvious.

Because of this, I've always been very self-conscious about my weight. For as long as I can remember I *have* been skinny, but I've never felt skinny enough. Sometimes I run in place before bed to burn a few calories, sometimes I sleep on my arm in hopes that that'll stop any fat from growing past it, but usually I just punch my stomach when in the shower and give away my lunch to everyone else, desperately hoping that will be enough.

I could live with quietly suffering about my body, if it weren't for the fact that despite everything in the world telling me it's wrong, I *like* fat men.

I'm not the only one either, hundreds of people in the gay community feel the same way that I do. Though, considering my family calls people like them freaks, it doesn't make me feel much better.

I kept it a hidden secret for years, before finally, in 9th grade, I told my friend Morgan. She laughed for awhile before realizing I was serious, and then proceeded to try and make up for it by searching for #teenfatguys in the instagram tags. As you can probably expect, nothing came up, but the entire concept of it lasted and became such a big thing in my mind that it managed to be the title of what you're reading right now, as well as a common joke in my friend group.

Because of this, roughly everyone of my friends knows about it by now, which is nice since most don't openly judge, but also horrible because if I ever talk about boys at my house, I'm met with the constant fear that they might accidentally bring it up.

We'd be casually talking about some cute guys, or girls if they're into that, and then they'd ask, *So you don't like boobs, right?*

"Yeah."

Oh no wait, you like boobs just not girl boobs.

And then a force stronger than an earthquake would shake the house as my mom runs up the stairs to scream and question my friend about what they meant by that. And trust me, when Cynthia gets mad, she's relentless, and would not stop until my friend breaks down and confirms that yes, Jake is attracted to fat guys.

But why? My mom would cry, *They're so large and… pudgy.*

"Yeah," I'd sigh dreamingly, "They are."

What, does that mean you want to be fat too!?

"Pretty much."

And then I'd be locked in the attic for the rest of my life.

In all seriousness, it should never matter what other people think about your body *or* the body you're attracted to. What matters is your own preference, and if anyone tries to take that away from you, you should always fight against it. And mom, dad, if you're reading this…

I'd like my tombstone to say: R.I.P. T.F.G.

THOUGHTS

4/3/16

My ceiling seems so boring at first glance, probably because it is, but I like it. It looks clean. And smooth. But if you look at it for more than three seconds you can tell there's more going on.

There's nine small, almost invisible cracks, five tiny holes, an uncountable amount of dents, one smoke alarm, one vent, and a fan.

I just realized today just how much time I spend looking at my ceiling. Too much. Because instead of working, or procrastinating, I kinda just stare up and try to not think about anything. It's kinda like when your body feels like it's about to vomit, and your throat keeps moving around as if to say, *I'm ready, feel free to puke any time!* But you don't want to run to the nearest toilet out of fear for not making it, so instead you just lay down and wait for it to go away. Except in this case it doesn't go away, so you're just suck staring at the ceiling the whole time.

But my ceiling is so cool! It's like a mirror without glass, constantly staring back without eyes as if the paint it still drying even though it already did years ago.

4/4/16

There's actually ten cracks in my ceiling, I just found another one.

[Drawing of the crack, in purple]

SHRINKING SIZES

I don't wear pajamas often. That's a weird way to start a story, but it's true.

Typically, when I go to sleep, I wear the same clothes I had worn that day. It doesn't matter if they're uncomfortable. It doesn't matter if they get wrinkled. It doesn't matter if the buttons on my shirt press into my chest so much that they leave marks. All that matters, is that I don't have to get changed multiple times each day.

On the rare occasion that I do wear pajamas, they're always the same ones. A pair of sweatpants that are a size too big, and an old Padres shirt that's been around since before I was born. It's old, it's blue, and it smells kinda strange, but if I don't wear it, no one will.

A few weeks ago, I wore pajamas for what may have been the first time in a year. When I pulled the shirt over my head, I expected it to be longer than it actually was. I searched through my pajama drawer for a few minutes, wondering if I had somehow pulled out the wrong shirt.

I hadn't.

When I stood in front of one of the door sized mirrors we have in our house and looked at myself, I realized how much older I really was.

I was no longer small enough to wrap a pillow case around myself and tape it so it looked like a skirt. I could no longer wear my mother's high heels like clown boots. I don't grow so fast that I have to send out old clothes every month anymore. And this shirt, this completely average sized shirt doesn't seem like a dress on me anymore.

I don't know what it's like to wake up from a coma and see yourself years older than you were before, but if I had to guess, I think it would feel something like that.

I must have stared at myself for hours, pulling down so that the neckline stretched out. I desperately tried to make myself smaller, but with each passing second, I seemed to grow. As I slowly moved my elbows into my sleeves, my mind repeated the same thought.

This shirt used to go down to my knees.

This shirt used to go down to my knees.

But it doesn't anymore.

And it never will again.

THOUGHTS

2/4/17

I can't sleep. I don't know the last time I got more than 3 hours of it at a time, and the space around my eyes has turned so purple that it looks like I slowly let some lumberjack press logs into my eyes till they bruised.

2/6/17

I'm so tired. I think I'm going to start writing down that I can't sleep every night that I can't from now on.

2/7/17

I can't sleep.

2/8/17

I can't sleep.

2/11/17

I can't sleep.

2/12/17

I can't sleep.

2/13/17

I can't sleep.

2/15/17

I can't sleep.

2/16/17

I can't sleep.

[Drawing of a bed]

2/17/17

I can't sleep.

2/18/17

This isn't working very well so I'm going to write down when I can sleep instead.

2/21/17

I slept.

2/22/17

I slept.

3/1/17

I slept.

3/2/17

I slept.

3/3/17

I slept.

3/25/17

I slept.

3/26/17

I'm giving up.

NO TEARS SHAMPOO

When I was a child, I had two states of being. I was either **A)** Your average little kid, or **B)** A human waterfall. Everything in the world made me burst into tears. If I tripped and fell, tears. If I heard something that was a bit too loud, tears. If my brother fell, tears. If I got a shot, surprisingly no tears. In fact, shots were the only thing that would make my brother turn into a living fountain instead of me, though that's not my story to tell.

The constant crying, caused by a combination of both little emotional control and a strange level of eye pressure I inherited from my mother, eventually drove my family insane. So, one fateful day, my mother led me over to the creepy part of the kitchen next to the basement, bent over till she was face to face with my five year old self, and said, *Jacob, sweetie, you need to stop fucking crying.* My small brain interpreted this as, *I'm very mad at you, your brother is a million times better than you in every way, except when it comes to taking shots, and now we're sending you off to live alone.* Naturally, I started crying. And after my mother finished covering her ears, she promised she would give me a dollar for every day I didn't cry.

I earned a grand total of one dollar.

As time went on, I continued to change. I gained more control over how I felt, stopped getting into physically painful situations, and wore goggles in the shower so no shampoo would get in my eyes. 3 years passed quickly. In those years, my knowledge expanded, my creativity deepened, and my hair grew down to my shoulders into a disgusting mess of dirt and tangles.

I spent the majority of those years with the same three kids. My brother, my best friend, and my best friend's brother. Our two families often met to eat dinner, so as the adults discussed adult topics like taxes and health care, we retreated upstairs and into a box filled with costumes and toy weapons. As the democratically raised kids we were, we all voted for which game we wanted to play that day. 3 for war, 1 for house. Can you guess who voted for house?

We always split into two teams, younger brothers v.s. older brothers, but the older brothers always won. Maybe that was because they were smarter, or stronger, or because I hid behind my bed the entire time, who really knows? It didn't matter in long run, because I would always end up in tears before the game was done. One specific day, I had fallen in my friends garage, and as I sat there with my knee bleeding and my eyes blurry, I heard my brother whisper, *Has anyone noticed that we always have to stop playing because Jake gets hurt?* It was just a stupid comment from an annoyed child, but I stopped crying around them after that.

Elementary school continued as it normally did, with little to nothing changing as the years went on. I still worked decently hard, though I was nothing special when compared to the other kids in my class. While many of them got to go get a free popsicle for being a good student, I had to stay behind in my overly large 4th grade classroom with no natural sunlight. I was determined to get my own free popsicle, and the one time I did, I was too late getting down the stairs, and the very grumpy lunch lady refused to give me a popsicle despite the fact that the box was in her hands, and yes, I'm still mad.

This was supposed to be a proud moment, and to me, it was a devastating blow. Naturally, I started crying as I slowly made my way back up the stairs. My teacher asked me what was wrong, and I didn't want to seem like a wimp, so I lied and said a kid tripped me. You know, something that only happens to the cool kids.

I met with the school counselor every day that week because of that, and I just continued lying, because now if I told the truth, I'd get that head shake of disapproval and a letter for my parents. They did still get a letter, though that one said to talk to me and find out if I was getting bullied. I guess it was an effective letter, because they still ask me to this day, despite the fact that the answer never changes.

My transition into middle school was awkward. Not puberty awkward, just socially awkward. All the kids I used to playfully push onto cement and then play wall ball with went to a different school than me, so I was forced to talk to the kids who I knew, but didn't know. In an effort to seem approachable, since approaching was out of the question, I smiled so much my braces bent.

For 3 years I was that overly excited kid. I was so happy in middle school that at one point, my really tall friend bent down to look me in the eyes, and told me to start feeling bad, because I was intimidating him. But I didn't stop being overly happy, because people liked me, and that felt great.

I didn't want anyone to know it was an act. And luckily for me, no one figured it out. Like most teenagers, I was dealing with a lot of personal problems all at once. I was comparing myself to my brother, questioning my sexuality, and freaking out over how much I weighed. My face was pristine porcelain, but my brain was a shit storm. And I refused to let that show.

In my mind, a single tear became something that could tear my life apart, but in reality, the only thing the two have in common, is the spelling.

I realized this freshman year of high school after a long argument with my brother. He yelled at me, I pretended I didn't care, and once he left, I stood on the edge of my roof, stared at the ground below, and wondered what would happen if I jumped. More tears fell from my eyes that day than every day of middle school combined. Water filled my mouth when I screamed, my hands hurt when I hit them against the wall, and once I had climbed under the covers of my bed, my entire body was filled with relief.

30 days into my junior year of high school, I had the astounding realization that I had no idea what I was doing. I had figured out my sexuality, thank god, but my comparisons to my brother only grew, while the weight problem remained the same, and the addition of school stress snuck its way onto the list. But all of that was okay. Because the next morning, when I took my shower, little bits of shampoo washed into my eyes.

Naturally, I started crying.

THOUGHTS

What I know:

1. Wisdom and child-like freedom aren't tied down by age. If you want to be the dancing queen after the age of seventeen, you can.

2. There are people who love you, and there are people you love, but they aren't always the same. Stick with the people who fit into both.

3. Immortality is achievable, but only through hearts and minds.

4. Just ignore destiny. It's dumb.

5. It is impossible to help others at the expense of yourself. If what you are doing hurts you, then you aren't helping anyone.

6. Categories exists to define, but there isn't a single thing in the universe that only fits into one. You are larger than A, B, or C, and when you run out of letters, make a new one.

7. You shouldn't sugar coat the words you speak. No matter how hard something is to swallow, we all have strong intestines.

8. You are not evil, but you are not good. You are not needed, but you are not worthless. You are simply you. And that is a great thing to be.

9. Life is worth living.

   Do it.

ALL EYES ON ME

On the first day of my junior year of high school, my new english teacher, Ms. Beltran, informed us that at the beginning of every day, we would dance. This, was terrifying. I don't see myself as a good dancer at all, and so the entire concept of, *hey you need to dance in front of 30 other kids as well as the teacher you'll be with for a year*, is probably one of the worst things you can hear on the first day of school.

I don't like it when people look at me, for the most part, and so usually I don't present much, and when I have to dance in front of others, I try to keep everything as simple as possible so I sort of look like I know what I'm doing. But Ms. Beltran is an interesting teacher. I'm not sure *how* but she found a way to make everyone dance together and present *when they want to* without anyone switching out or deciding to abuse the system by not doing either.

Learning, for the first time in a long time, was interesting for the whole year. Everything was interactive since we shared our opinions on it, but it also moved quickly and was straightforward, even when it was supposed to be complicated. Plus, we always learned about something new, since on fridays we got to give a presentation on *whatever we wanted to.*

As someone who is far too interested in way too many things, this pushed me to start actually presenting whenever I could. It was still terrifying, but when I gave my presentation on 'Mouth Sounds,' a mashup album where almost every song features 'All Star,' I felt strangely powerful when everyone laughed with me.

And the fact that the next morning we danced to 'All Star' helped too.

The funny thing about dancing, is that no one cares if you look like an idiot, because they're dancing too, and in most cases, they also look pretty stupid. It's the same with presenting, some people will judge you based on how much your hands shake or how many *ums* you mutter, but most people will just listen to what you have to say and worry about how if *they* were up there, they would be doing *much worse.*

So when I gave my 'TED Talk' at the end of the year, I wasn't completely terrified, and I didn't have to worry about dancing after we had all finished either. Because the moment 'All Star' came on, and Ms. Beltran pushed me to the center of the room, I danced with everyone watching.

And for the first time, I didn't mind.

THOUGHTS

Dear Me,

Life's a bitch. I have no idea what you could possibly be going through right now, mostly because it hasn't happened yet, but I hope everything turns out well. Today is June 12, 2017, and I'm sitting on my bed alone just two days before the school year is over. Time has been going by so fast, and I'm sure that by the time you're reading this you'll feel like you just put it in an envelope a few seconds ago.

There are so many things I want to say and not enough words to say them with. Sure, I could fill this up with questions about the future, things like *Did Kingdom Hearts 3 come out?* or *Is Spongebob canceled yet?* but what's the point if I'll never get a response? Don't answer that. I already know there isn't one.

Instead, I have hopes and advice, things both obvious and forgettable, so you'll probably need to be reminded of them by now.

Hold onto those that you care about. I know it's hard, and that the people you love will come and go, but look at whoever is there now and stand by them. You need them, and whether you choose to believe it or not, they need you too.

Keep yourself alive. This seems like a dumb thing to say, but I don't mean stay alive in a physical sense. Of course you should keep breathing, not doing so would ruin everything you and I have worked towards all these years. *I still may not know what that is, but maybe you do. And even if you don't, it's still there.* What I really meant by keeping yourself alive was more in terms of personality and thought. Are you healthy enough to function normally? If they put your mind in a program, would you be an interesting AI? Do you contradict yourself from earlier and add questions despite saying you wouldn't before? If the answer is no to any of these, or yes to the last one, then take a break and try to bring yourself back, because right now he's probably lost, and scared, and not in the same place you left him.

My last piece of advice is keep writing. Writing probably still seems intimidating, and it is, but you've always needed it, and you still do. There are so many ideas in your head. Put them down before they fly away.

I hope you feel better while reading this, or smarter, or larger, or anything for that matter. I hope you've gained a few pounds. I hope you published that book. I hope you've found yourself a cute boy. I hope that when you look in the mirror you are able to see someone worth seeing. I hope you're happy, or getting there, or figuring it out. I hope you look back on this in a year, or two, or five, and get closer and closer to wherever you decided you want to be.

I want to say you're going to go far, but we both know that there's no way to know if you will or not. What I do know is that I think of you every day, and I know that usually it's out of hatred or disgust, but good god deep down I love you.

I love you so much.

Sincerely,

You.

Made in the USA
Monee, IL
07 July 2026

56544285R00103